# The Early Career of the Prophet Jeremiah

# The Early Career of the Prophet Jeremiah

JACK R. LUNDBOM

WIPF & STOCK · Eugene, Oregon

Dedicated with affection to

*Fredrick C. Holmgren*

and

*F. Burton Nelson*

My teachers at
North Park Theological Seminary

THE EARLY CAREER OF THE PROPHET JEREMIAH

Copyright © 2012 Jack R. Lundbom. All rights reserved. Except for brief quotations in critical publications or reviews, no part of this book may be reproduced in any manner without prior written permission from the publisher. Write: Permissions, Wipf and Stock Publishers, 199 W. 8th Ave., Suite 3, Eugene, OR 97401.

Wipf & Stock
An Imprint of Wipf and Stock Publishers
199 W. 8th Ave., Suite 3
Eugene, OR 97401
www.wipfandstock.com

Originally published by Mellen Biblical Press (Lewiston/Queenston/Lampeter). Copyright Edwin Mellen Press, 1993.

ISBN 13: 978-1-62032-541-4
Manufactured in the U.S.A.

# Contents

*Abbreviations*     ix
*Preface*     xi
*Introduction*     xv

1. An Early Career Beginning before the Reform:
   *The Traditional View*     1
2. A Career Beginning after the Reform:
   *Challenges to the Traditional View*     40
3. An Early Career Beginning at the Height of the Reform:
   *A New View*     55
4. A Trajectory of Jeremiah's Early Career     67

   *Bibliography*     85
   *Scripure Index*     91

# Abbreviations

| | |
|---|---|
| AB | The Anchor Bible |
| ABD | The Anchor Bible Dictionary |
| ATD | Das Alte Testament Deutsch |
| BA | The Biblical Archaeologist |
| BDB | Brown, Driver Briggs, *A Hebrew and English Lexicon of the Old Testament* (Oxford, 1906) |
| BETL | Bibliotheca Ephemeridum Theologicarum Lovaniensium |
| BJRL | Bulletin of the John Rylands Library |
| BK | Biblischer Kommentar |
| BWAT | Beiträge zur Wissenschaft vom Alten Testament |
| CB | The Century Bible |
| CBC | The Cambridge Bible Commentary |
| CBQ | Catholic Biblical Quarterly |
| CBSC | Cambridge Bible for Schools and Colleges |
| CTM | Concordia Theological Monthly |
| EncB | Encyclopaedia Britannica |
| EncJud | Encyclopaedia Judaica (Jerusalem, 1971) |
| ET | Expository Times |
| HAT | Handbuch zum Alten Testament |
| HKAT | Handkommentar zum Alten Testament |
| HTR | Harvard Theological Review |
| IB | Interpreter's Bible |
| ICC | International Critical Commentary |

*Abbreviations*

| | |
|---|---|
| IDB | Interpreter's Dictionary of the Bible |
| Int | Interpretation |
| ITC | International Theological Commentary |
| JBC | The Jerome Biblical Commentary |
| JBL | Journal of Biblical Literature |
| JNES | Journal of Near Eastern Studies |
| JSOT | Journal for the Study of the Old Testament |
| KAT | Kommentar zum Alten Testament |
| KHC | Kurzer Hand-Commentar zum Alten Testament |
| LXX | Greek Septuagint |
| MT | Hebrew Masoretic Text |
| NEB | New English Bible |
| NICOT | New International Commentary on the Old Testament |
| NKZ | Neue Kirchliche Zeitschrift |
| NRSV | New Revised Standard Version |
| OTL | Old Testament Library |
| OTM | Old Testament Message |
| RB | Revue Biblique |
| REB | Revised English Bible |
| RSV | Revised Standard Version |
| SBLDS | Society of Biblical Literature Dissertation Series |
| SBU | Svensk Bibliskt Uppslagsverk |
| SEÅ | Svensk Exegetisk Årsbok |
| TBC | Torch Bible Commentaries |
| TGUOS | Transactions of the Glasgow University Oriental Society |
| TOTC | The Tyndale Old Testament Commentaries |
| VT | Vetus Testamentum |
| WBC | Word Biblical Commentary |
| WMANT | Wissenschaftliche Monographien zum Alten und Neuen Testament |
| ZAW | Zeitschrift für die alttestamentliche Wissenschaft |

# Preface

THE MAIN THESIS OF this book, presented in chapter 3, developed gradually following the completion of my doctoral dissertation, *Jeremiah: A Study in Ancient Hebrew Rhetoric* (1975).[1] That work was in rhetorical criticism, and as such dealt with historical and chronological problems only as they came up. I was not after anything approaching a definitive solution to Jeremiah's early career. The chronology given in the book seemed to me to be secure, and I found myself more or less in agreement with those who posited an early career beginning in "the 13th year of Josiah" (1:2). Yet it was clear to me, even then, that the early career as commonly mapped out presented problems. Just how difficult the problems were I knew not, but the realization came once I began working on solutions.

Anyone reading the Jeremiah commentaries knows how many pages are given over to a discussion of chronology—chronology of the prophet's career and chronology, or its lack, of oracles and other materials making up the book of Jeremiah. The reasons are not hard to find. Dates are all but nonexistent in chapters 1–20, but even more important, the chapters following 1–20 contain *so many* chronological indicators of various description that scholars are teased, as it were, into sketching for this prophet what they sketch for no other prophet in the Hebrew Bible, save perhaps Isaiah: a career. Early in the century, therefore, biblical scholars despite their differences on a range of key issues did reach a consensus of sorts on the career of the prophet Jeremiah.

---

1. SBLDS 18; Missoula, MT: Society of Biblical Literature and Scholars Press, 1975.

*Preface*

At the same time, for nearly a century now, a dedicated group of scholars has refused to join the consensus, maintaining that the chronology in the book must be revised downward. Solutions advanced by these individuals have not met with wide acceptance, nevertheless, the questions they raise in search for better answers continue to be discussed, and make for lively debate even today when the issue of Jeremiah's career comes up for review.

For many current scholars the problem of Jeremiah's career is reduced in importance—for some set aside entirely—in part, because of the shift away from historical-critical scholarship as it has been understood and practiced for two centuries or more. Many in fact would argue that the book's message can be grasped with or without historical underpinnings, or, that exegesis and interpretation can proceed apace with or without literary-critical judgments. In the case of Jeremiah, historical questions are de-emphasized or put aside simply because the solutions arrived at by an earlier generation of scholars no longer command assent. So Jeremiah's career, even in these instances, remains a problem, only here a problem scholars prefer not to address.

The present work takes issue with those who want to jettison historical-critical scholarship. That is simply not an option, in this writer's opinion. It also takes issue with those who hasten on with exegesis and interpretation without addressing literary-critical issues. Offering as it does a new solution to the problem of Jeremiah's early career, it builds on the twin assumptions that scholarship in the modern or post-modern era must continue its quest for a historical background to the message of this great prophet, no matter how imperfect the reconstruction might be, and that literary-critical issues in the book of Jeremiah are as important as they have always been. Some arguments in the work derive from insights gained through rhetorical criticism. These do not render unnecessary work carried on in other critical disciplines. The aim of rhetorical criticism in relation to other critical disciplines is to confirm, supplement, or, if need be, correct.

*Preface*

The present work expands a lecture given at Uppsala University on May 28, 1985. A portion of my argument on that occasion, that having to do with chapter 1 of Jeremiah, has been published as "Rhetorical Structures in Jeremiah 1," *ZAW* 103 (1991), 193-210. My thanks to Agge Carlson and Helmer Ringgren who invited me to Uppsala for that occasion, and who, together with colleagues, discussed the lecture in a high seminar later that day. The exchange was both stimulating and helpful. What is now presented incorporates subsequent reflections, which, I hope, will answer some of the questions raised in that seminar.

Scripture passages, except as otherwise noted, are those of the *New Revised Standard Version* (NRSV) of the Bible.

Lutheran School of Theology at Chicago
June 1993

# Introduction

FOR MORE THAN A century Old Testament scholars committed to historical and literary-critical investigation of the Bible have sketched out, in broad outline at least, a career for the prophet Jeremiah. This sketch has been part of a broader quest to recover the historical Jeremiah, also world events of the late 7th and early 6th cc. B.C. against which the ministry of the prophet might properly be viewed.

Historical and literary-critical investigation of the Bible are rooted in the Renaissance and Protestant Reformation. Both were nurtured subsequently by the Enlightenment which gave birth to a modern critical mentality in the West. This came to flower in what may now be called the New Renaissance of the 19th and 20th cc., a time when all branches of Near Eastern studies, fed by archaeological work begun when Napoleon opened up Egypt in 1799 and troops discovered the Rosetta Stone, impacted the modern world in the way classical studies impacted Italy and the rest of Europe in the 15th and 16th cc. In the past two centuries the West has also had direct contact with peoples of the Near East, further contributing to this New Renaissance.

In the late 19th c. it was fashionable to write "biographies" of ancient biblical personages. New Testament scholars for some time had been producing biographies of Jesus, based, for the most part, on materials gleaned from the four gospels. In the case of the Old Testament prophet Jeremiah writing a biography was facilitated by generous amounts of historical and biographical information in the book of Jeremiah, supplemented by portions of 2 Kings and 2 Chronicles which reported the Josianic Reform

*Introduction*

and Judah's fall to the Babylonians. Added to all of this were the many extra-biblical texts now becoming available, most notable of which were the historical texts of the late Assyrian Age found in the library of Ashurbanipal at Nineveh, and the Babylonian Chronicle. Writing a biography of Jeremiah could therefore be undertaken with a reasonable measure of confidence, so it was thought, at least with more confidence than with any other prophet. For the other Hebrew prophets the task was unthinkable, except perhaps for Isaiah of Jerusalem where supporting materials were available, though in lesser amounts.

Not all who wrote biographies of Jeremiah were as candid as T. K. Cheyne, who, in his book, *Jeremiah: His Life and Times* (1888), said such an effort was possible only with "the help of the imagination."[1] Cheyne was a critical scholar, not overly influenced by 19th c. romanticism which is what provided the impulse for most of those writing their ancient "lives". He did the "Jeremiah" article for the celebrated 11th ed. of the *Encyclopaedia Britannica*.

The optimism of 19th c. scholars who thought they could write biographies of ancient biblical personages faded early in the present century. Source critics of the Wellhausen era, and even more the form critics who came later, recognized that chronology did not control the collection of biblical materials as much as had been previously thought, nor did ancient historical writing possess the precision of modern historical writing. Duhm and Cornill concluded that the book of Jeremiah seldom gave up unambiguous historical and biographical data. Greater skepticism was expressed with respect to the former.

With the coming of form criticism and its agenda of discerning literary genres (Gunkel: *Gattungen*), some Jeremiah scholars have argued that prose in chapters 21-45 of the book is not biography, but "saga" or "legend."[2] Gunkel, however, did not

1. (London: James Nisbet & Co., 1888), 13-14.
2. See Martin Kessler, "A Prophetic Biography: A Form-Critical Study of Jer. 26-29, 32-45" (Unpublished PhD dissertation, Brandeis University, 1965);

consider this prose legend, saying it contained no magical deeds about Jeremiah and was "extraordinarily faithful."[3] Muilenburg, another giant in form criticism, affirmed much the same.[4] The results then of form criticism in Jeremiah study have been mixed. But it is true that Jeremiah scholars no longer call any part of the Jeremiah book "biography" in the modern sense, nor would they suggest that anyone today be capable of writing a modern Jeremiah biography.

An undisguised "anti-historical" stance is taken in the works of many current Jeremiah scholars, most notably Nicholson, McKane, and especially Carroll in Great Britain,[5] and Thiel along with his mentor Herrmann in Germany, for whom the historical Jeremiah recedes into the hoary past and the focus is almost entirely on the late "Deuteronomic" redaction of the book.[6] This is largely the legacy of Duhm. These individuals take the bulk of the Jeremianic material as emanating from the exilic and post-exilic periods. There are, of course, important differences in the works of these scholars, still, none is much interested in mapping out a career for the prophet Jeremiah.

---

*idem*, "Form-Critical Suggestions on Jer 36," *CBQ* 28 (1966), 390; Klaus Koch, *The Growth of the Biblical Tradition* (tr. S. M. Cupitt; New York: Charles Scribner's Sons, 1969), 201–205 with qualification. See further the comments in my *Jeremiah: A Study in Ancient Hebrew Rhetoric*, 13 (1997: 23–24).

3. H. Gunkel, "The Secret Experiences of the Prophets," *The Expositor* 9th Series 1 (1924), 434.

4. J. Muilenburg, "Baruch the Scribe" in *Proclamation and Presence* (eds. John I. Durham and J. R. Porter; Richmond: John Knox Press, 1970), 233.

5. E. W. Nicholson, *Preaching to the Exiles: A Study of the Prose Tradition in the Book of Jeremiah* (New York: Schocken Books, 1971); William McKane, *Jeremiah* 1 (ICC; Edinburgh: T. & T. Clark, 1986); Robert P. Carroll, *From Chaos to Covenant* (New York: Crossroad, 1981); *idem, The Book of Jeremiah* (OTL; Philadelphia: Westminster Press, 1986).

6. Winfried Thiel, *Die deuteronomistische Redaktion von Jeremia 1–25* (WMANT 41; Neukirchen-Vluyn: Neukirchener Verlag, 1973); *idem, Die deuteronomistische Redaktion von Jeremia 26–45* (WMANT 52; Neukirchen-Vluyn: Neukirchener Verlag, 1981). S. Herrmann, *Jeremia* (BK 12:1-2; Neukirchen-Vluyn: Neukirchener Verlag, 1986–1990), *idem, Jeremia: Der Prophet und das Buch* (Darmstadt: Wissenschaftliche Buchgesellschaft, 1990).

*Introduction*

A different situation obtains with the American scholars John Bright and William L. Holladay. Bright, besides being a Jeremiah scholar, is a historian of ancient Israel. On literary-critical questions he is more the form-critic. While Bright agrees that a biography of Jeremiah can no longer be written, he does think it possible, at least in a general way, to reconstruct the prophet's career.[7] The same goes for William Holladay,[8] whose literary-critical views combine the older source criticism with newer stylistic and rhetorical criticism. Both scholars, in any case, venture to sketch a career for the prophet Jeremiah.

The two reconstructions, however, could not be more different. Bright holds to what may be called the "traditional view," which accepts the chronology in the book of Jeremiah and posits an early career in the reign of Josiah. Holladay argues that the chronology of the traditional view is too high, and lowers it. This has the practical result of eliminating an "early career" and confining Jeremiah's ministry almost entirely to the reigns of Jehoiakim and Zedekiah. Needless to say, each reconstruction has implications for the interpretation of the Jeremianic message, not to mention what sort of profile emerges of the historical Jeremiah and what background can be assumed for the ministry he had.

Four major questions present themselves to anyone wishing to sketch out an early career for the prophet Jeremiah: 1) When does Jeremiah receive his call, and how old is he at the time? 2) Does any Jeremianic preaching date from the late Assyrian Age? 3) What relation does Jeremiah have, if any, to the Josianic Reform? and 4) Who is the "foe from the north" mentioned early in the book?

We turn now to discuss each of these questions as they have been addressed by those holding the traditional view of Jeremiah's early career.

7. John Bright, *Jeremiah* (AB 21; Garden City, NY: Doubleday & Co., 1965), lxxxvi-lxxxvii.

8. William L. Holladay, *Jeremiah* 1 (Hermeneia; Philadelphia: Fortress Press, 1986), 1–10; *Jeremiah* 2 (Hermeneia; Minneapolis: Augsburg Fortress, 1989), 25–35.

# 1

# An Early Career Beginning before the Reform: The Traditional View

## THE DATE OF THE CALL AND JEREMIAH'S AGE

ACCORDING TO THE TRADITIONAL view Jeremiah receives a call, accepts it, and begins his ministry as a prophet of Yahweh in the 13th year of King Josiah. This view builds to a large extent on the chronology in the book, and to a lesser extent on the interpretation of chapter 1. The book's superscription says,

> ¹The words of Jeremiah son of Hilkiah, one of the priests who were in Anathoth in the land of Benjamin, ²to whom the word of the LORD came in the days of King Josiah son of Amon of Judah, in the thirteenth year of his reign. (1:1–2)

At the beginning of chapter 25 we also read,

> ¹The word that came to Jeremiah concerning all the people of Judah, in the fourth year of King Jehoiakim son of Josiah of Judah (that was the first year of King Nebuchadrezzar of Babylon), ²which the prophet Jeremiah spoke to all the people of Judah and all the inhabitants of

## The Early Career of the Prophet Jeremiah

> Jerusalem: ³For twenty-three years, from the thirteenth year of King Josiah son of Amon of Judah, to this day, the word of the LORD has come to me, and I have spoken persistently to you, but you have not listened. (25:1–3)

The key date here is the 13th year of Josiah, 627 B.C., which is five years before the book of the law was found in the temple and the reform activities of 2 Kings 22–23 were carried out. From the perspective of the Deuteronomic Historian the entire reform took place in the year 622.[1]

The superscription of 1:1–3 is of particular importance to the traditional view, for which reason it has been the subject of much discussion. Some suggest it was affixed to the book by a contemporary, perhaps Jeremiah's scribal friend Baruch. Others say it comes from a later time, and may in fact be a composite. In either case, the date contained in v 2—together with dates derived from 25:1–3—are the oldest tradition we have telling us when the word of Yahweh first came to Jeremiah. That word was the call which follows in 1:4–10. The formulaic statement introducing the call in v 4, is believed to refer back to v 2 of the superscription which mentions the 13th year of Josiah.[2] This connection is what anchors the call in Josiah's 13th year.

The chronological data in 25:1–3 are believed to suggest an early career lasting 23 years, beginning when the call was received and extending to the 4th year of Jehoiakim. The dates are 627–605 B.C.[3] The following year, 604 B.C.,[4] a collection of

---

1. The chronological reckoning in scholarly works dating back three decades or more was 626 B.C. for the call of Jeremiah and 621 B.C. for the reform.

2. So John Calvin, *Commentaries on the Book of the Prophet Jeremiah and the Lamentations I* (Grand Rapids: Baker Book House, 1979), 33–35; F. Giesebrecht, *Das Buch Jeremia* (HKAT; 2nd ed.; Göttingen: Vandenhoeck & Ruprecht, 1907), 2; B. Duhm, *Das Buch Jeremia* (KHC; Tübingen and Leipzig: Verlag von J. C. B. Mohr [Paul Siebeck], 1901), 4; and C. H. Cornill, *Das Buch Jeremia* (Leipzig: Chr. Herm. Tauchnitz, 1905), 3.

3. The early career may be extended to 604 (36:9 MT), which is when the scroll is read in the temple and Jeremiah and Baruch go into hiding.

4. The MT of 36:9 says "fifth" year of Jehoiakim, but the LXX reads "eighth"

## An Early Career Beginning before the Reform: The Traditional View

the prophet's words was read publicly in the temple and privately before the king (36:9-26). Jeremiah, like his predecessor Isaiah, is seen to close an initial phase of public ministry by preparing a scroll of important prophecies, after which he enters forced retirement (36:19, 26; cf. Isa 8:16-17).

Those holding the traditional view include Calvin, and such modern scholars as C. B. Michaelis, J. D. Michaelis, F. Hitzig, K. H. Graf, F. Giesebrecht, B. Duhm, C. H. Cornill, P. Volz, F. Nötscher, A. Weiser, and W. Rudolph of Germany; C. von Orelli of Switzerland; I Engnell of Sweden; S. Mowinckel and H. Birkeland of Norway; E. Henderson, T. K. Cheyne, S. R. Driver, A. S. Peake, A. W. Streane, J. Skinner, T. H. Robinson, G. A. Smith, A. Welch, H. Freedman, H. H. Rowley, H. Cunliffe-Jones, and R. E. Clements of Great Britain; A. Condamin of France; J. A. Thompson of Australia; J. M. Berridge, R. K. Harrison, and P. Craigie of Canada; and J. A. Bewer, C. C. Torrey, J. Muilenburg, E. A. Leslie, J. Bright, T. Overholt, and L. Boadt of the United States.[5] These scholars do not of course agree on details of the

---

year. Lohfink and Holladay follow the LXX; see N. Lohfink, "Die Gattung der 'Historischen Kurzgeschichte' in den letzten Jahren von Juda und in der Zeit des Babylonischen Exils," *ZAW* 90 (1978), 324-328; W. L. Holladay, "The Years of Jeremiah's Preaching," *Int* 37 (1983), 150-151; *idem, Jeremiah I*, 4. Bright (*Jeremiah*, 182) adopts the MT reading, noting that precisely in December, 604 the Babylonian army was present in the Philistine plain sacking Ashkelon. Such an event would explain the need to proclaim a national day of fasting in Jerusalem.

5. Calvin, *Jeremiah and Lamentations I*, 27; Christian B. Michaelis, *Prolegomena in Ieremiam Prophetam* (Halle: Litteris Hendelianis, 1733); Johann D. Michaelis, *Observationes Philologicae et Criticae in Jeremiae Vaticinia et Threnos* (Göttingen: Vandenhoeck & Ruprecht, 1793); F. Hitzig, *Der Prophet Jeremia* (2nd ed.; Leipzig: Verlag von S. Hirzel, 1866); K. H. Graf, *Der Prophet Jeremia* (Leipzig: T. O. Weigel, 1862); F. Giesebrecht, *Das Buch Jeremia*; B. Duhm, *Das Buch Jeremia*; C. H. Cornill, *Das Buch Jeremia*; Paul Volz, *Der Prophet Jeremia* (KAT; 2nd ed.; Leipzig: A. Deichertsche Verlagsbuchhandlung, D. Werner Scholl, 1928); F. Nötscher, *Das Buch Jeremias* (Bonn: Peter Hanstein Verlagsbuchhandlung, 1934); A. Weiser, *Das Buch Jeremia 1-25,13* (ATD 20; 8th ed.; Göttingen: Vandenhoeck & Ruprecht, 1981); W. Rudolph, *Jeremia* (HAT; 3rd ed.; Tübingen: J. C. B. Mohr [Paul Siebeck]. 1968); C. von Orelli, *The Prophecies of Jeremiah* (tr. J. S. Banks; Edinburgh: T. & T. Clark, 1889); I. Engnell,

## The Early Career of the Prophet Jeremiah

early career, nor also the course which Jeremiah's ministry took from the time of the call to 604 B.C. But all share the view that the call came in the 13th year of Josiah, i.e., 627 B.C., and that in this year also Jeremiah accepted his call and began straightaway a public ministry on behalf of Yahweh God.

Two other verses, 3:6 and 36:2, mention "the days of Josiah" in connection with Jeremiah's ministry. The wording of 36:2, "from the days of Josiah until today," resembles 25:3. "Today" is

---

"Jeremias bok" in *SBU* 1 (2nd ed.), 1098; S. Mowinckel, *Zur Komposition des Buches Jeremia*(Oslo: Jacob Dybwad, 1914); H. Birkeland, *Zum Hebräischen Traditionswesen: Die Komposition der prophetischen Bucher des Alten Testaments* (Oslo: Jacob Dybwad, 1938); E. Henderson, *The Book of the Prophet Jeremiah and That of the Lamentations* (London: Hamilton, Adams and Co., 1851); T. K. Cheyne, *Jeremiah: His Life and Times*; S. R. Driver, *The Book of the Prophet Jeremiah* (London: Hodder & Stoughton, 1906); A. S. Peake, *Jeremiah I* (CB; New York: Henry Frowde, and Edinburgh: T. C. & E. C. Jack, 1910); A. W. Streane, *The Book of the Prophet Jeremiah together with the Lamentations* (CBSC; Cambridge: Cambridge University Press, 1913); John Skinner, *Prophecy and Religion* (Cambridge: Cambridge University Press, 1922); T. H. Robinson, *Prophecy and the Prophets in Ancient Israel* (London: Duckworth, 1923); George Adam Smith, *Jeremiah* (4th ed.; New York and London: Harper & Bros., 1929); Adam C. Welch, *Jeremiah: His Time and His Work* (Oxford: Oxford University Press, and London: Humphrey Milford, 1928 [reprint Westport, CT: Greenwood Press, 1980]); H. Freedman, *Jeremiah* (Soncino; London: Soncino Press, 1949); H. H. Rowley, "The Early Prophecies of Jeremiah in Their Setting," *BJRL* 45 (1962–63), 198–234 [reprint in L. G. Perdue and B. W. Kovacs eds., *A Prophet to the Nations: Essays in Jeremiah Studies* (Winona Lake, IN: Eisenbrauns, 1984), 33–61]; H. Cunliffe-Jones, *The Book of Jeremiah* (TBC; London: SCM Press, 1960); R. E. Clements, *Jeremiah* (Interpretation; Atlanta: John Knox Press, 1988); Albert Condamin, *Le Livre de Jérémie* (3rd ed.; Paris: Librairie Lecoffre, 1936); J. A. Thompson, *The Book of Jeremiah* (NICOT; Grand Rapids: William B. Eerdmans Publishing Co., 1980); John M. Berridge, *Prophet, People, and the Word of Yahweh* (Zürich: EVZ-Verlag, 1970); R. K. Harrison, *Jeremiah and Lamentations* (TOTC; Downers Grove, IL: Inter-Varsity Press, 1973); Peter C. Craigie et al., *Jeremiah 1–25* (WBC 26; Dallas: Word Books, 1991); J. A. Bewer, *The Book of Jeremiah I* (New York: Harper & Bros., 1951); C. C. Torrey, "The Background of Jeremiah 1–10," *JBL* 56 (1937), 193–216; James Muilenburg, "Jeremiah the Prophet" in *IDB*, E–J, 823–835; Elmer A. Leslie, *Jeremiah* (New York and Nashville: Abingdon Press, 1954); John Bright, *Jeremiah*; Thomas W. Overholt, "Some Reflections on the Date of Jeremiah's Call," *CBQ* 33 (1971), 165–184; Lawrence Boadt, *Jeremiah 1–25* (OTM9; Wilmington, DE: Michael Glazier, 1982).

the 4th year of Jehoiakim. The verse 3:6 introduces a passage of uncertain length with the words: "The LORD said to me in the days of King Josiah:" This notation is unusual, for with the exception of the chronological indicators in 1:2 and 1:4, nowhere else in chapters 1–20 is a date attached to an utterance or activity of Jeremiah. The lack of dates in chapters 1–20 is indeed the chief obstacle to sketching out an early career. About that we will say more later.

We get practically no help in documenting the early career from other sources. The Chronicler tells us that Jeremiah uttered a lament at the funeral of Josiah (2 Chr 35:25), which was 609 B.C., but since a majority of earlier scholars downplayed Chronicles as a historical source, this mention was downplayed, for some disregarded entirely. Bright's more positive appraisal of the Chronicler reflects a shift of opinion which came with Albright and his students.[6] From extra-biblical sources contemporary with Jeremiah no relevant information is available.

In the call passage we are told that Jeremiah was a *naʿar* when Yahweh first spoke to him about being a prophet (1:6–7). A *naʿar* is a "young male," one who might be in infancy, but more commonly a boy of 10 or 12, otherwise in the late teens. Joseph is a *naʿar* at 17 (Gen 37:2), and Josiah a *naʿar* at 16 but apparently not at 20 (2 Chr 34:3). Solomon refers to himself as a *naʿar* after he has become king and is married (1 Kgs 3:7). But we are not told how old he is at the time. The term, however, does extend into the upper range of chronological age, for in the Bible *naʿar*

---

6. See W. F. Albright, "The Biblical Period" in *The Jews: Their History, Culture and Religion I* (ed. Louis Finkelstein; rev. ed., New York: Harper and Bros., 1955), 42–45; Frank M. Cross Jr. and David Noel Freedman, "Josiah's Revolt against Assyria," *JNES* 12 (1953), 56–58; and Werner E. Lemke, "The Synoptic Problem in the Chronicler's History," *HTR* 58 (1965), 349–363. An earlier appraisal of the Chronicler more positive in nature came from Adam C. Welch, *The Work of the Chronicler* (London: British Academy and Oxford University Press, 1939). This fine work has not received the attention it deserves. See now also Berridge, *Prophet, People, and the Word of Yahweh*, 21. The negative assessment of the Chronicler can be traced back to de Wette; see Sara Japhet, "The Historical Reliability of Chronicles," *JSOT* 33 (1985), 83–107.

describes not only young men of marriageable age, but soldiers and slaves (BDB, 655). Here in 1:6–7 the RSV translates *na'ar* "youth" which a happy compromise between infancy and adulthood. The NRSV, however, changes to "boy". Most scholars holding the traditional view push Jeremiah's age up as far as possible in order that he be at a reasonable level of maturity when his public career begins. Some put his age at 23–25, which would mean that he was born ca. 650.[7] A smaller number prefer an age of 18, which puts his birth at ca. 645.[8]

Up through the end of the 19th c. it was assumed that chapter 1 comprised a unified composition, reporting a single experience in the life of the prophet. That experience was Jermiah's call to be a prophet and his commission to begin ministry. A new perspective, however, came in the works of Bernhard Duhm and Sigmund Mowinckel. Both claimed that the superscription in v 11 signaled a new beginning, which had the practical effect of reducing Jeremiah's call experience to just vv 4–10. The two visions—delimited to vv 11–16—were bracketed out as separate experiences brought in by a later editor. The commission was reported in vv 17–19, but agreement was never reached whether this belonged to the call or constituted a separate experience. There are more serious problems with this reconstruction, about which we will say more when we come to discuss the structure of chapter 1.

---

7. Duhm, *Jeremia*, 3; Cornill, *Jeremia*, 6; G. A. Smith, *Jeremiah*, 66; Peake, *Jeremiah I*, 3; Condamin, *Jérémie*, 3; Volz, *Jeremia*, xi; Nötscher, *Jeremias*, 5; Weiser, *Jeremia 1–25*, 13, 10; and Rudolph, *Jeremia*, iii.

8. Skinner, *Prophecy and Religion*, 24; Bewer, *Jeremiah I*, 11; and Bright, *Jeremiah*, xxix. Among the older commentators one will also meet up with dates based on different calendar calculations, e.g., F. Hitzig, *Der Prophet Jeremia*, x, and Henderson, *Jeremiah and Lamentations*, vi, who place the 13th year of Josiah at 629 B.C. Henderson (p. 2) puts Jeremiah's age at 20, giving him a birth date of 649.

*An Early Career Beginning before the Reform: The Traditional View*

## REFLECTIONS OF THE LATE ASSYRIAN AGE

If Jeremiah begins his prophetic career in 627 B.C., he is thrust into public life precisely at the point when his nation—indeed the entire world—is undergoing tumultuous change. These are the last days of the mighty Assyrian empire.

The rapid demise of Assyria is understood today in some detail, thanks to the discovery of Assyrian historical texts from Nineveh and elsewhere, the Babylonian Chronicle, and other important archaeological finds such as the Haran Inscription which fixes the date of Ashurbanipal's death at 627 B.C.[9] But the basic scenario could be perceived just by reading between the lines of the biblical record in 2 Kgs 21:19–23:37.

We know that Assyria was severely weakened by war during the 650s, but nevertheless survived. Psammetichus I of Egypt, for example, declared his independence in 655. The empire continued to be in a state of rebellion until Ashurbanipal regained a measure of control in 640. Following Ashurbanipal's death, in October, 626, Nabopolassar defeated the Assyrian army outside Babylon and declared himself King of Babylon. From this point on it was downhill for Assyria. In 612 Nineveh fell to a coalition of Babylonians, Medes, and the Umman-Manda.[10] Two years later Haran fell. The Assyrian attempt to retake Haran in 609, which brought Egypt into the fray on the side of the Assyrians, failed utterly. An age was ended.

For Judah any joy felt over the demise of Assyria was mingled with sorrow, because Josiah was killed at Megiddo trying to stop Neco's march north and eastward. But before this tragedy, while

---

9. See William W. Hallo, "From Qarqar to Carchemish: Assyria and Israel in the Light of New Discoveries," *The Biblical Archaeologist Reader II* (eds. David Noel Freedman and Edward F. Campbell; Garden City, NY: Doubleday & Co., 1964), 187; also John Bright, *A History of Israel* (3rd ed.; Philadelphia: Westminster Press, 1981), 315. Henri Cazelles, "Zephaniah, Jeremiah, and the Scythians in Palestine" in Perdue and Kovacs 1984: 133, puts the end of Ashurbanipal's reign` ca. 630 B.C.

10. C. J. Gadd, *The Fall of Nineveh* (London: British Museum, 1923).

## The Early Career of the Prophet Jeremiah

Assyria was faltering in faraway Mesopotamia, Judah had three happy decades of political and religious freedom. Independence was declared *de facto* in 640 when the pro-Assyrian Amon was killed and Josiah put on the Jerusalem throne. Nationalism had been rekindled and vast changes occured, the most significant of which was the religious reform described in 2 Kings 22–23 and 2 Chronicles 34–35.

Those holding the traditional view imagine that Jeremiah was active—or at least that an early career as a prophet was being lived out—during the final 18 years of the Assyrian decline, i.e., 627–609 B.C. But documenting these years with his preaching and other activity is another matter, mainly because the material in chapters 1–20 and 30–31—thought to be the earliest in the book—is undated. Scholars therefore are left to infer from the content of this material what Jeremiah was preaching about and what other things he was doing during the late Assyrian Age.

In 2:18 and 2:36 mention is made of Assyria. These verses also mention Egypt, which, for the traditional view takes on added importance in that Egypt and Assyria are the powers still to be reckoned with during Josiah's time. In Josiah's final years they became allies in the fight against Babylon.

The first of these verses occurs in a passage commonly delimited to 2:14–19.[11] It reads:

> [14]Is Israel a slave? Is he a homeborn servant?
> Why then has he become plunder?
>
> [15]The lions have roared against him
>   they have roared loudly
> They have made his land a waste
>   his cities are in ruins, without inhabitant
> [16]Moreover, the people of Memphis and Tahpanhes
>   have broken the crown of your head
> [17]Have you not brought this upon yourself

---

11. So H. Gunkel, "Schriftstellerei und Formensprache der Propheten" in *Die Propheten* (Göttingen: Vandenhoeck & Ruprecht, 1917), 117–118.

> by forsaking the LORD your God
> while he led you in the way?
>
> ¹⁸What then do you gain by going to Egypt
> to drink the waters of the Nile?
> Or what do you gain by going to Assyria
> to drink the waters of the Euphrates?
> ¹⁹Your wickedness will punish you
> and your apostasies will convict you
> Know and see that it is evil and bitter
> for you to forsake the LORD your God
> the fear of me is not in you
> says the LORD God of hosts.

The passage begins with rhetorical questions that call attention to the nation's lamentable condition, badly battered is it by enemy attacks, in direct contrast to earlier days in the wilderness when Israel as Yahweh's bride was well-protected (2:2–3).[12] The lions of v 15 are past armies, very likely Assyrian armies such as the one which laid Samaria waste in 722 B.C., or the one which ravaged Judah in 701 B.C. leaving Hezekiah in Jerusalem "like a bird in a cage."[13] Some holding the traditional view, however, think that the attackers are more recent.[14]

In v 16 the enemy is clearly Egypt ("the people of Memphis and Tahpanhes"), though agreement has not been reached on how the verb *yir'ûk* should be translated. It is an imperfect, but the RSV and NRSV translate it as a past. The NEB and REB take it as a future (REB: "the people of Noph and Tahpanhes will break your heads"). Commentators are equally divided.[15] Much

---

12. Duhm, *Jeremia*, 21–22.
13. Ibid., 22; Peake, *Jeremiah I*, 93; S. R. Driver, *Jeremiah*, 14; Streane, *Jeremiah and Lamentations*, 13; Bewer, *Jeremiah I*, 14; Rudolph, *Jeremia*, 19; Bright, *Jeremiah*, 17; and Thompson, *The Book of Jeremiah*, 172–173.
14. The Scythians, for example, who roamed Asia in the 7th c. leaving much destruction in their wake; so Skinner, *Prophecy and Religion*, 56 n.1.
15. Those taking the verb as a future include Calvin, C. B. Michaelis, *Prolegomena in Ieremiam Prophetam*, 17; Henderson, *Jeremiah and Lamentations*, 12; Duhm, *Jeremia*, 22–23; Streane, *Jeremiah and Lamentations*, 14; Skinner,

of the debate centers on whether the verse alludes to Neco's defeat of Josiah at Megiddo in 609. Many believe it does. A judgment regarding this, also the tense of the verb, have consequences for dating the passage. For those holding the traditional view 609 is the *terminus ad quem* for Assyria being a world power.

Assyria and Egypt are mentioned explicitly in v 18, where the leaders of Judah are being chided for a current foreign policy ill-conceived, one which seeks help from Egypt and then from Assyria. The main point of the passage taken as a whole is that Judah, by relying on these nations, has abandoned Yahweh and his covenant. But, as we mentioned, the issue so far as Jeremiah's early career is concerned is whether the references to Assyria and Egypt in v 18 are an indication that the passage derives from the late Assyrian Age.

It is also not clear from the passage whether Assyria and Egypt are rival powers or allies. If they are rival powers, then Judah is vacillating politically, unable to make up its mind which nation to choose for an ally. Hosea mocked Israel for precisely this sort of behavior (Hos 7:11). Rival political parties would account for such a vacillation,[16] a reality Jerusalem by now was accustomed to.[17] The bitter fruit of this sort of foreign policy was well-known, for promised help often did not come (2 Chr 28:16–21 in the case of Assyria). So if Assyria and Egypt were rivals, a date prior to 616 for v 18 is required, because when the Babylonian Chronicle picks up in 616 after a hiatus of a few years, Egypt and Assyria have joined forces and are now fighting a common enemy.[18]

---

*Prophecy and Religion*, 56 n.1; Weiser, *Jeremia*, 18; Rudolph, *Jeremia*, 18–19; and Berridge, *Prophet, People, and the Word of Yahweh*, 75. A lesser number of scholars take it as a past; see G. A. Smith, *Jeremiah*, 94; Bright, *Jeremiah*, 9.

16. Bright, *Jeremiah*, 14.

17. So Calvin, *Jeremiah and Lamentations I*, 101; Streane, *Jeremiah and Lamentations*, 15.

18. Gadd, *The Fall of Nineveh*, 6–7.

*An Early Career Beginning before the Reform: The Traditional View*

It is of course possible that v 18 reflects neither rival powers abroad nor rival factions at home, but a coalition party in Judah which is pressing for a united front against the advancing Babylonians. In this case, Jeremiah would be speaking out against such a policy, and a date between 616 and 609 would be suitable. But v 18 cannot be dated after 609, for then Assyria is being sought out by no one. Some scholars do, however, date portions of vv 14–19 later than 609—usually v 16 because it calls to mind Josiah's death at the hands of Neco.[19] Many who hold the traditional view date v 18 between 627 and 622, judging vv 14–19 to be a unity and taking chapter 2 as a whole to be Jeremiah's preaching immediately after his call.[20]

The second reference to Assyria and Egypt in 2:36 reads:

> How lightly you gad about
> changing your ways!
> You shall be put to shame by Egypt
> as you were put to shame by Assyria.

Much of what has just been said about v 18 applies also here, although in this verse the indictment is not for vacillating back and forth. Judah has changed (Heb *šannôt*) foreign policy—away from Assyria in the direction of Egypt. If Egypt and Assyria are competing powers, then like v 18 this verse must also be dated prior to 616.[21] But since a political shift toward Egypt was forced upon Judah in 609 when Neco placed Jehoiakim on the throne (2 Kgs 23:34), v 36 would fit perfectly well after 609. But again,

---

19. Those taking v 16 as a post-609 interpolation include G. A. Smith, *Jeremiah*, 94; S. R. Driver, *Jeremiah*, 9; Bewer, *Jeremiah I*, 14; Rudolph, *Jeremia*, 19; and Bright, *Jeremiah*, 14. Others, e.g., Cornill, *Jeremia*, 21; Peake, *Jeremiah I*, 92–93; and Streane, *Jeremiah and Lamentations*, 13, because they believe there to be a link between v 13 and v 18, take all of vv 14–17 as a later interpolation.

20. See Skinner, *Prophecy and Religion*, 44–45 n.3; 56 n.1. Bright, *Jeremiah*, lxxiv, 16–18, thinks that v 18 shows Assyria still to be a world power, but says that the material achieves its present form after 609; see also Berridge, *Prophet, People, and the Word of Yahweh*, 75.

21. J. Milgrom, "The Date of Jeremiah, Chapter 2," *JNES* 14 (1955), 65–69, says the verb *šannôt* means "change".

scholars holding the traditional view commonly date v 36 with the rest of the chapter, i.e., between 627 and 622 B.C. Specific events have been suggested as possible background, but many simply concede they do not know what Jeremiah had in mind here.[22]

Another passage said to reflect the late Assyrian Age is 13:1–11, the incident about the buried waistcloth. It reads:

> [1]Thus says the LORD to me, "Go and buy yourself a linen loincloth, and put it on your loins, but do not dip it in water." [2]So I bought a loincloth according to the word of the LORD, and put it on my loins. [3]And the word of the LORD came to me a second time, saying, [4]"Take the loincloth that you bought and are wearing, and go now to the Euphrates, and hide it there in a cleft of the rock." [5]So I went, and hid it by the Euphrates, as the LORD commanded me. [6]And after many days the LORD said to me, "Go now to the Euphrates, and take from there the loincloth that I commanded you to hide there." [7]Then I went to the Euphrates, and dug, and I took the loincloth from the place where I had hidden it. But now the loincloth was ruined; it was good for nothing. [8]Then the word of the LORD came to me: [9]"Thus says the LORD: Just so I will ruin the pride of Judah and the great pride of Jerusalem. [10]This evil people, who refuse to hear my words, who stubbornly follow their own will and have gone after other gods to serve them and worship them, shall be like this loincloth, which is good for nothing. [11]For as the loincloth clings to one's loins, so I made the whole house of Israel and the whole house of Judah cling to me, says the LORD, in order that they might be for me a people, a name, a praise, and a glory. But they would not listen.

---

22. Calvin, *Jeremiah and Lamentations I*, 148, cites events from the reign of Hezekiah. Skinner, *Prophecy and Religion*, 45 n, thinks this verse, like 2:18, alludes to appeals for help against the Scythians. Bewer, *Jeremiah I*, 17, says the verse is to be interpreted against the background of the death of Ashurbanipal. Peake, Streane, and Bright say the events are unknown.

## An Early Career Beginning before the Reform: The Traditional View

In this passage Jeremiah is told by Yahweh to buy a new linen waistcloth, wear it briefly, and then go "to *Perat*" (Heb *pĕrātāh*) where he is to bury it. "*Perat*" (Heb *pĕrāt*) is the Euphrates (cf. LXX), the river upon which the Assyrian nation lies. Again the word comes to Jeremiah to go to *Perat*, this time to retrieve the buried cloth. Jeremiah does so, and with feigned surprise he announces that the cloth is spoiled. The lesson in all of this: Judah's pride will be spoiled on account of its chasing after other gods. This theme, lacking only the dress of stereotyped prose, dominates Jeremiah's early preaching of chapters 2–3.

If one is to take the account literally, Jeremiah before the object lesson is complete will have made two roundtrips of 700 miles each to the Euphrates, one to bury the cloth and a second to retrieve it. Not surprising then that commentators for a long time have opted for a non-literal interpretation, some taking the passage as a vision, others as an allegory. Duhm, because the passage is Deuteronomic prose, gives it a late date and considers it unhistorical. One interpretation which has been successful in gaining adherents calls attention to the fact that in Hebrew the spelling of "to *Perat*" is the same as "to Parah", and Parah (Heb *pārāh*) is a known location four miles distant from Anathoth, Jeremiah's home (cf. Josh 18:23). The suggestion is therefore made that Jeremiah's destination for the waistcloth burial is nearby Parah rather than the distant Euphrates.[23] The possibility also of a double meaning for *Pĕrātāh* would give the symbolic act added richness: Jeremiah, by going to Parah, simulates a trip to the Euphrates, or Assyria (cf. 2:18).

If this action is intended to be an indictment of Assyria and her gods, then a date prior to 609 is required for reasons already stated. Since Haran is situated on the Euphrates, and the Assyrians made their last stand here between 612 and 610, the incident

---

23. Peake, *Jeremiah I*, 191–192 quotes with approval the earlier suggestion by Schick; see also G. A. Smith, *Jeremiah*, 184 and Bright, *Jeremiah*, 96. It has been pointed out, however, that this explanation accounts only for the usage with *he locale* in vv 4, 6 and 7, and not for *biprāt* in v 5; cf. McKane, *Jeremiah I*, 285.

could date from that time. The incident would of course make perfectly good sense earlier in Josiah's reign, and that is where some place it.[24] Others, however, assign it to the reign of Jehoiakim.[25] The poetry following in vv 15–27 is dated just prior to the exile of 597, and because of this some think Jeremiah's action is pointing to exile.[26] Whether or not there are allusions here to exile has been much debated. Perhaps the connection with Judah's exile is made only later when compilation of the material takes place.

In chapters 30–31, within the so-called "Book of Comfort," Jeremiah alternately addresses "Jacob" (30:10, 18; 31:7, 11) and "Ephraim" (31:9, 18, 20) with a message of hope. Upon these people in "the land of the north" (31:8) the favor of Yahweh is said to rest, and they are invited to return to Zion. Who are these people? Most likely "the remnant of Israel" (31:7) or the remnant of the old Northern Kingdom which ceased to be after 722 B.C. when Assyria took Samaria. These people could be those living in and around Samaria (cf. 41:5), otherwise exiles still at a more northerly location in Assyria. In either case the invitation is being extended for them to come joyfully to Jerusalem. A typical passage of lyric poetry in this collection is 31:2–14:

> [2]Thus says the LORD:
> The people who survived the sword
>     found grace in the wilderness
> when Israel sought for rest
>     [3]the LORD appeared to him from far away
> I have loved you with an everlasting love
>     therefore I have continued my faithfulness to you
> [4]Again I will build you, and you shall be built
>     O virgin Israel!

---

24. Cornill, *Jeremia*, 171, and somewhat more tentatively Peake, *Jeremiah I*, 10.

25. T. H. Robinson, *Prophecy and the Prophets*, 123; G. A. Smith, *Jeremiah*, 183. Rudolph, *Jeremia*, 94, says the passage could be dated either before the reform or in the time of Jehoiakim, but in either case before 597 B.C.

26. Bright, *Jeremiah*, 95–96; cf. discussion in McKane, *Jeremiah I*, 288–292.

Again you shall take your tambourines
    and go forth in the dance of the merrymakers
[5] Again you shall plant vineyards
    on the mountains of Samaria
the planters shall plant
    and shall enjoy the fruit
[6] For there shall be a day when sentinels will call
    in the hill country of Ephraim:
"Come, let us go up to Zion
    to the LORD our God."

[7] For thus says the LORD:
Sing aloud with gladness for Jacob
    and raise shouts for the chief of the nations
proclaim, give praise, and say
    "Save, O LORD, your people
    the remnant of Israel"
[8] See, I am going to bring them from the land of the north
    and gather them from the farthest parts of the earth
among them the blind and the lame
    those with child and those in labor, together
    a great company, they shall return here
[9] With weeping they shall come
    and with consolations I will lead them back
I will let them walk by brooks of water
    in a straight path in which they shall not stumble
for I have become a father to Israel
    and Ephraim is my firstborn.

[10] Hear the word of the LORD, O nations
    and declare it in the coastlands far away
say, "He who scattered Israel will gather him
    and will keep him as a shepherd keeps his flock"
[11] For the LORD has ransomed Jacob
    and has redeemed him from hands too strong for him
[12] They shall come and sing aloud on the height of Zion
    and they shall be radiant over the goodness of the LORD
over the grain, the wine, and the oil
    and over the young of the flock and the herd
their life shall be like a watered garden
    and they shall never languish again

> ¹³Then shall the young women rejoice in the dance
>     and the young men and the old shall be merry
>   I will turn their mourning into joy
>     I will comfort them, and give them gladness for sorrow
> ¹⁴I will give the priests their fill of fatness
>     and my people shall be satisfied with my bounty
>       says the LORD.

All the poetry in the Book of Comfort is undated. Nevertheless, it is argued by some that this passage, along with others in the collection expressing hope, were originally spoken to exiles who had survived the deportation to Assyria. That the passages were later intended to sustain those who went to exile in Babylon goes without saying, but an earlier audience is imagined, and thus an earlier date for the prophecies. An earlier date would place the passages in Josiah's reign, when Judah was rife with excitement over Assyrian weakness and nationalistic sentiments were carrying the day. Many therefore date the passages early.²⁷

Such a call for the exiles to return from Assyria may be possible after 609, when Assyria is powerless and Babylon is in position to decide the fate of displaced persons, except that following Josiah's death optimism at home vanished, and the poetry here literally teems with hope and optimism for the future. Another reason for dating the passages early is Jeremiah's use of "Ephraim" for Israel. This betrays influence from Hosea, and that influence is thought to have shown itself early in Jeremiah's career.²⁸

Another passage earlier in the book calls people to return from the north. It is found in 3:12–18. A core of poetry in vv 12–13 (some say vv 12–14) summons northern Israelites to return

---

27. For both chapters 30–31: Volz, *Jeremia*, 277–302; Rudolph, *Jeremia*, 188–189; and G. P. Couturier, "Jeremiah" in *JBC*, 325; for chapter 31 only: Peake, *Jeremiah I*, 10; Bright, *Jeremiah*, xci, 284–285; T. M. Ludwig, "The Shape of Hope: Jeremiah's Book of Consolation," *CTM* 39 (1968), 526–541; and E. Lipinski, "Jeremiah" in *EncJud* 9, 1347.

28. Skinner, *Prophecy and Religion*, 21; Muilenburg, "Jeremiah the Prophet" in *IDB*, 825; and Rudolph, *Jeremia*, 188–189. See also the works of Karl Gross cited in note 36.

to Yahweh—also to Zion if v 14 be included. What follows in vv 14–18 is expansion, most likely from the exilic period.[29] The core poetry in 3:12–13, together with its superscription, reads:

> [12]Go, and proclaim these words toward the north, and say:
> Return, faithless Israel
>     says the LORD
> I will not look on you in anger
>     for I am merciful
>         says the LORD
>     I will not be angry forever
> [13]Only acknowledge your guilt
>     that you have rebelled against the LORD your God
> and scattered your favors among strangers under every green tree
>     and have not obeyed my voice
>         says the LORD.

This passage is dated early for the same reason as the hope passages in chapters 30–31, viz., that northern Israel is being addressed and a word about exiles returning from the north is likely to have been spoken during the late Assyrian age. Also, if this poetry in vv 12–13 falls under the rubric of 3:6, which gives a date in the days of Josiah, we have confirmation of it being early. But there are scholars holding the traditional view who question an early date for the prose in vv 6–11,[30] which may or may not affect an early date for vv 12–13.

---

29. Verse 15 cannot date from the time of Josiah since it presupposes the incompetency of those presently holding office, and Jeremiah is known to have admired Josiah; see Bewer, *Jeremiah I*, 19. Verse 18 also post-dates Josiah because Judah has now joined Israel in exile.

30. Some argue that this parable of the two adulterous sisters is dependent upon Ezekiel 16 and 23. Bright (*Jeremiah*, 26–27) rejects that view, saying the verses have their closest affinities to Hosea and the Jeremianic poetry. He therefore dates vv 6–13 to Josiah's reign, vv 14–15 somewhat later, and vv 16–18 to the exilic period.

# The Early Career of the Prophet Jeremiah

## JEREMIAH AND THE JOSIANIC REFORM

Instability within the Assyrian empire meant new political freedom for Judah, and with political freedom came the opportunity to effect sweeping changes in the religious life of the nation. That opportunity was seized, with the result that Judah underwent what was undoubtedly its most extensive reform ever. It happened while Josiah was king.

The Josianic Reform[31] is recorded in 2 Kings 22–23 and 2 Chronicles 34–35, and only there. It receives no explicit mention in the book of Jeremiah. The accounts in Kings and Chronicles differ in certain important respects.[32] In Kings the entire reform—including the purge of idolatrous practices in the south and in the north—is a consequence of the lawbook's discovery in 622 B.C. In Chronicles the reform takes place in stages and begins earlier. The purge of the land comes in 628 (2 Chr 34:3b-7), six years *before* the lawbook is discovered.

Scholars by and large have shown a decided preference for the account in 2 Kings,[33] which means that attempts by those holding the traditional view to map out an early career for Jeremiah are done against this background. One will commonly hear scholars of an earlier generation refer to "the reform of 622/1", as if everything happened in that one year.[34] Also, the call

---

31. I prefer the term "Josianic Reform" to "Deuteronomic Reform" for two reasons: 1) there is a need to distinguish between the reforms of Hezekiah and Josiah, both of which were connected in some fashion with the book of Deuteronomy; and 2) I want to disassociate myself from the view that Deuteronomy or proto-Deuteronomy (i.e., chapters 12–26 or 5–26, 28) was the lawbook found in the temple in 622 B.C. I believe the lawbook was the Song of Moses in Deuteronomy 32; see my article, "The Lawbook of the Josianic Reform," *CBQ* 38 (1976), 293–302.

32. "The Lawbook of the Josianic Reform," 294–295.

33. A qualified acceptance of the Chronicler's account may be seen in Cheyne, *Jeremiah: His Life and Times*, 16–17, and H. H. Rowley, "The Prophet Jeremiah and the Book of Deuteronomy" in *Studies in Old Testament Prophecy* (ed. H. H. Rowley; Edinburgh: T. & T. Clark, 1950), 164–165. On the more positive appraisal of the Chronicler later on, see further note 6.

34. See e.g., Skinner, *Prophecy and Religion*, 63, 91; also H. H. Rowley, "The

## An Early Career Beginning before the Reform: The Traditional View

for obedience to the Mosaic covenant, the purge of the land, and the move to have worship centralized in Jerusalem—are all perceived as direct responses to mandates contained in the lawbook, which is believed to be an early version of our present book of Deuteronomy.

One must go again to undated material in the book of Jeremiah in search of evidence for a relationship between Jeremiah and the Josianic Reform. If allusions to the above-stated themes, to other material in Deuteronomy, or to the book itself can be found in certain passages, then these passages can be anchored in Josiah's reign and Jeremiah can be found either supporting or acting in opposition to the reform—but only after 622, because that is when the lawbook becomes public and the reform program begins.

The preaching in chapters 2–3 is about religious harlotry on a national scale, a theme believed to dominate reform rhetoric generally in 622. But this particular preaching, however, is said to be earlier, i.e., immediately after the call of 627.[35] Jeremiah is breaking up the fallow ground of the Manasseh period (4:3b), preparing the nation without either of them knowing it for the climactic events of 622. It is a common assumption—though not always stated in so many words—that Jeremiah's mandate to attack idolatrous worship comes directly and exclusively from Yahweh; what mobilizes the king into action, against the very same evil, is the newly-found lawbook. There is, however, one acknowledged influence upon the young Jeremiah, and that is

---

Early Prophecies of Jeremiah," 200.

35. Bright, *Jeremiah*, xc, 16–17, 25–26, though he qualifies his judgment by saying that the material received its present form in the reign of Jehoiakim. Many commentators date all of chapters 1–6 (or 2–6) between 627 and 622; cf. Peake, *Jeremiah I*, 10–11; S. R. Driver, *Jeremiah*, xxvii, 5; and Berridge, *Prophet, People, and the Word of Yahweh*, 74. C. C. Torrey in "The Background of Jeremiah 1–10," argued that all of chapters 1–10 represented Jeremiah's message prior to 622, although he believed a single author wrote the chapters in the third century B.C.

the preaching of Hosea which develops the theme of the adulterous wife.[36]

Jeremiah's earliest preaching in chapters 2–3 takes place during a period of general tranquility, when no military threat is imminent.[37] A typical passage reflecting this lack of turbulence is said to be 2:5–13:

> [5]Thus says the LORD:
> What wrong did your ancestors find in me
>    that they went far from me
> and went after worthless things
>    and became worthless themselves?
> [6]They did not say, "Where is the LORD
>    who brought us up from the land of Egypt
> who led us in the wilderness
>    in a land of deserts and pits
> in a land of drought and deep darkness
>    in a land that no one passes through
>    where no one lives?"
> [7]I brought you into a plentiful land
>    to eat its fruits and its good things
> But when you entered you defiled my land
>    and made my heritage an abomination
> [8]The priests did not say, "Where is the LORD?"
>    Those who handle the law did not know me
> the rulers transgressed against me
>    the prophets prophesied by Baal
>    and went after things that do not profit.
> [9]Therefore once more I accuse you
>      says the LORD
>    and I accuse your children's children.
>
> [10]Cross to the coasts of Cyprus and look
>    send to Kedar and examine with care

---

36. On the indebtedness of Jeremiah to Hosea see Karl Gross, *Die literarische Verwandtschaft Jeremias mit Hosea* (Inaug. diss.; Borna-Leipzig: Universitätsverlag von Robert Noske, 1930); *idem*, "Hoseas Einfluss auf Jeremias Anschauungen," *NKZ* 42 (1931), 241–256, 327–343.

37. Skinner, *Prophecy and Religion*, 54–55; Bright, *Jeremiah*, 26.

>       see if there has ever been such a thing
>    ¹¹Has a nation changed its gods
>       even though they are no gods?
>    But my people have changed their glory
>       for something that does not profit
>    ¹²Be appalled, O heavens, at this
>    be shocked, be utterly desolate
>       says the LORD
>    ¹³for my people have committed two evils:
>    they have forsaken me
>    the fountain of living water
>       and dug out cisterns for themselves
>    cracked cisterns
>       that can hold no water.

In 3:1 we have what appears to be a clear reference to the law in Deut 24:1–4 which regulates remarriage. It reads:

>    If a man divorces his wife
>       and she goes from him
>    and becomes another man's wife
>       will he return to her?
>    Would not such a land be greatly polluted?
>    You have played the whore with many lovers
>       and would you return to me?
>          says the LORD.

If Jeremiah is quoting the law of Deuteronomy, which seems likely, then he would appear to be supporting the reform since Deut 24:1–4, according to those holding the traditional view, is part of the 622 lawbook. The argument for dependence has problems, however, and most of those holding the traditional view do not use it. The reason is that the poetry in chapter 3 is commonly dated between 627 and 622, which means the lawbook (containing Deut 24:1–4) is not yet available.[38] One needs to keep

---

38. Streane, *Jeremiah and Lamentations*, 21–22, notes the connection between 3:1 and Deut 24:1–4, but is not sure if Deuteronomy is yet in operation. Peake, *Jeremiah I*, 102, said earlier with regard to 3:1: "It is, however, very questionable whether there was any reference to Deut xxiv, 1–4, at least in the original text of the passage." Rowley, "The Prophet Jeremiah and the Book of

in mind that scholars of an earlier generation often continued to assume that the poetry in chapters 1–20 was in chronological order, more or less,[39] and that material in the larger groupings, e.g., 2:1–4:4; 4:5–6:30, were roughly of the same date.[40] Form criticism changed all this, and now each individual passage is dated on its own merits.[41]

If one were to single out a parade example of reform preaching in the early poetry, it would have to be the brief oracles in 4:1–4 which bring to an end the section on apostasy and idolatry.[42]

---

Deuteronomy," 171, takes an opposite view. He says: "That Jer. iii. 1 is to be connected with Deut xxiv. 1–4 is almost certain. It is improbable that Jer. iii. 1 is a post-Deuteronomic insertion in the text of Jeremiah, and equally improbable that Jeremiah was enunciating a principle which was afterwards accepted by the compilers of Deuteronomy and embodied in their Code. For apart from the fact that Jeremiah's originality was not as a lawgiver, he here appeals to a principle which was already known and accepted. It is therefore simplest to suppose that the text of Deuteronomy, where the principle is laid down, was already known." Bright, *Jeremiah*, 26, recognizes the connection but says nothing about dependence, assuming that the law is "assuredly more ancient" than its formulation in Deuteronomy.

39. Henderson, *Jeremiah and Lamentations*, xi-xii, seems to assume a "general consecutiveness" in chapters 1–20. G. A. Smith, *Jeremiah*, 16–17, 25–26, finds exceptions here and there, but it is Skinner, *Prophecy and Religion*, 54–56, 109, who makes a significant departure from the common view when he dates only a kernel of chapters 1–6 to the period between 627 and 622, and puts the oracles of chapter 2 *after* those of chapter 4. He also notes the jump from chapters 6 to 7, and the problem this creates for the poetry following chapter 7 if one holds firmly to chronological sequence.

40. Torrey, "The Background of Jeremiah 1–10," 195, argued that chapters 1–10 were in chronological order. More recently Milgrom, "The Date of Jeremiah, Chapter 2," 69, with minor qualification, concludes that chapters 1–6 are in chronological order. He says chapters 1–2 are pre-622 and chapters 3–6 simultaneous with and immediately subsequent to the reform.

41. The form-critical assumption of Bright (*Jeremiah*, lix) is stated straightforwardly: "No part of the Jeremiah book is arranged in chronological order, and any conclusions based upon the assumption that such is the case are false conclusions." Having said this, however, and also having concluded that portions of 2:1–4:4 reached their final form in Jehoiakim's reign or later, Bright nevertheless judges most of the material in the so-called "harlotry cycle" to be Jeremiah's earliest preaching between 627 and 622; see note 35.

42. Muilenburg, "Jeremiah the Prophet" in *IDB*, 825; Bright, *Jeremiah*, 25–26.

## An Early Career Beginning before the Reform: The Traditional View

Here Jeremiah calls for a return to Yahweh, a recommitment to truth and justice, and a circumcision of the heart:

> ¹If you return, O Israel
>   says the LORD
>   if you return to me
> If you remove your abominations from my presence
>   and do not waver
> ²and if you swear, "As the LORD lives"[43]
>   in truth, in justice, and in uprightness
> then nations shall be blessed by him
>   and by him shall they boast.
> ³For thus says the LORD to the people of Judah and to the inhabitants of Jerusalem:
> Break up your fallow ground
>   and do not sow among thorns
> ⁴Circumcise yourselves to the LORD
>   remove the foreskin of your hearts
> O people of Judah and inhabitants of Jerusalem
>   or else my wrath will go forth like fire
>   and burn with no one to quench it
>   because of the evil of your doings.

In 11:1–8 Jeremiah calls for obedience to the covenant, which is a reform theme if ever there was one. Shortly after the lawbook was found the king led the nation in a ceremony of covenant renewal (2 Kings 23). The interpretation of these verses, however, together with vv 9–17 which round out the larger prose unit, is complex. Verses 9–17 appear to post-date the death of Josiah when the reform had lapsed.[44] In v 9 it says a "revolt" or "conspiracy" (Heb *qešer*) is currently underway. This is a reaction thought to come from individuals who are hostile to the goals of the reform.[45] In v 10 it also says that people have "turned back" (Heb *šābû*) to prior iniquity, which again suggests a date

---

43. The translation of v 2a as apodosis is Bright's (*Jeremiah*, 21).
44. Peake, *Jeremiah I*, 179–180.
45. Henderson, *Jeremiah and Lamentations*, 74.

## The Early Career of the Prophet Jeremiah

in the reign of Jehoiakim when the covenant made by Josiah was repudiated.[46]

The earlier call for covenant obedience, however, fits well into the period immediately following 622.[47] 11:1–8 reads:

> ¹The word that came to Jeremiah from the LORD: ²Hear the words of this covenant, and speak to the people of Judah and the inhabitants of Jerusalem. ³You shall say to them, Thus says the LORD, the God of Israel: Cursed be anyone who does not heed the words of this covenant, ⁴which I commanded your ancestors when I brought them out of the land of Egypt, from the iron-smelter, saying, Listen to my voice, and do all that I command you. So shall you be my people, and I will be your God, ⁵that I may perform the oath that I swore to your ancestors, to give them a land flowing with milk and honey, as at this day. Then I answered, "So be it, LORD."
>
> ⁶And the Lord said to me: Proclaim all these words in the cities of Judah, and in the streets of Jerusalem: Hear the words of this covenant and do them. ⁷For I solemnly warned your ancestors when I brought them up out of the land of Egypt, warning them persistently, even to this day, saying, Obey my voice. ⁸Yet they did not obey or incline their ear, but everyone walked in the stubbornness of an evil will. So I brought upon them all the words of this covenant, which I commanded them to do, but they did not.

When Jeremiah is first called to set forth the terms of the covenant, he responds in the affirmative (vv 1–5).[48] The call

---

46. Bewer, *Jeremiah I*, 43.

47. Skinner, *Prophecy and Religion*, 101–103, following Erbt; see also Torrey, "The Background of Jeremiah 1–10," 195–197, 204.

48. The plural verb forms in v 2 are noted by Calvin as well as by more recent commentators--there are two if we read *dibbartem* instead of *dibbartām*. Jeremiah it seems has been commanded along with certain others to preach covenant obedience. Note also the plural verbs in the directive of 5:1.

comes again, and this time he reports that the effort was a failure (vv 6–8). Some think these are parallel accounts,[49] which would mean that Jeremiah is sent forth to preach his covenant message only once.

What scholars wonder about even more is precisely which covenant Jeremiah sets before the people. Is it the old Sinaitic covenant, or the recent covenant made by Josiah which was based on Deuteronomy? If it should be the latter, then Jeremiah is preaching on behalf of the reform. But some scholars point out that "this covenant" in vv 2–3 must refer ahead to vv 4–5 where the setting at Sinai is indicated.[50] Bright, who believes Jeremiah is referring here to Josiah's covenant, cautions nevertheless against making too sharp a distinction between the various covenants, for Josiah's covenant—also Deuteronomy, which is a covenant document—are but ratifications of the old Sinai covenant.[51] Yet it does matter whether or not Jeremiah is preaching on behalf of the reform.[52] Calvin, for whom the covenant was the entire law, noticed that the "cursed . . . amen" formula in vv 3–5 is the same one found in Deuteronomy 27. Subsequent scholars, for whom the link to Deuteronomy takes on even more importance, note this as well.[53]

The text itself has a built-in ambiguity with respect to the question of covenant. The LXX omits v 7 and all of v 8 except the very last words. It therefore reads:

49. Volz, *Jeremia*, 129.

50. Streane, *Jeremiah and Lamentations*, 76; and Skinner, *Prophecy and Religion*, 98 n.2, who points out that "this covenant" in vv 2–3 has no antecedent; see also Welch, *Jeremiah: His Time and His Work*, 95.

51. Bright, *Jeremiah*, 89.

52. Thompson, *Jeremiah*, 343, says: "The moment we are freed from the necessity of linking this passage with Josiah's lawbook and covenant based on it, we are under no obligation to regard the passage as coming from the days of Josiah."

53. Calvin, *Jeremiah and Lamentations II*, 74; Henderson, *Jeremiah and Lamentations*, 73, who says the phraseology in Jeremiah is borrowed from Deut 27:26; see also Duhm, *Jeremia*, 107; Streane, *Jeremiah and Lamentations*, 76; and Bewer, *Jeremiah I*, 43.

## The Early Career of the Prophet Jeremiah

> 6b  ... Hear the words of this covenant and do them
>
> 8b  But they did not do (them).

In the expanded MT there is the added reminder that generations from Sinai days up until the present have been warned about the importance of obedience. Yahweh then goes on to say that it became necessary to bring upon the people "all the words of this covenant" (v 8). In this particular context "words" is a polite term for "curses", and Yahweh most likely has in mind the curses of Deuteronomy 28. Scholars therefore judge the MT expansion to be exilic in origin.[54]

While many holding the traditional view see in this passage a tie-in between Jeremiah and the reform, for some an indication that Jeremiah supported the reform early in his career, nothing approaching a consensus has been reached on either point. Duhm and those sharing his negative assessment of the sermonic prose treat the whole passage as exilic theology without any historical basis.[55] For most others it boils down to whether Jeremiah preaches on behalf of the reform after 622,[56] or whether Jeremiah preaches covenant obedience only in Jehoiakim's reign when the reform is known to have lapsed.[57] Those who take the former

---

54. Skinner, *Prophecy and Religion*, 101–102, 328, who follows the lead of Erbt; see also Bright, *Jeremiah*, 89.

55. Duhm, *Jeremia*, 106–108; Cornill, *Jeremia*, 144. More recently Carroll, *From Chaos to Covenant*, 105, states: "The account in ch. 11 then represents an interpretation of the life of the prophet rather than a description of his real activities. It is an interpretation or presentation of Jeremiah in terms of deuteronomic theology. The prophet behaves as a perfect deuteronomist because to the deuteronomists that is how a prophet working in Josiah's time should behave."

56. Henderson, *Jeremiah and Lamentations*, vi; Peake, *Jeremiah I*, 11–14, though he wonders why Jeremiah needed to support a reform already being vigorously pursued by Josiah; G. A. Smith, *Jeremiah*, 143–146; S. R. Driver, *Jeremiah*, xxviii, 65; Skinner, *Prophecy and Religion*, 102–103; Rowley, "The Prophet Jeremiah and the Book of Deuteronomy," 171–174; Bewer, *Jeremiah I*, 43; and H. Freedman, *Jeremiah*, 80.

57. Streane, *Jeremiah and Lamentations*, 75–76; Bright, *Jeremiah*, 89.

## An Early Career Beginning before the Reform: The Traditional View

view separate out vv 1–8 (or vv 1–6, 8b) and date these verses early; those taking the latter view consider all of vv 1–17 to be preaching from the Jehoiakim years.

Earlier we discussed passages from chapters 3 and 30–31 which call for a return of exiles from the north, saying that such a call would fit well into the final years of Assyrian decline. Some of those same passages can now be examined in connection with a reform theme, viz., the centralization of worship at the Jerusalem temple. The destination of these returnees is Zion, which suggests to some Jeremiah's support of the centralization program which Josiah initiated after 622.[58] One such verse in 31:6 reads:

> For there shall be a day when sentinels will call
>    in the hill country of Ephraim:
> "Come, let us go up to Zion
>    to the LORD our God."

Unlike occurrences of "Zion" in passages of a similar nature, here the reference is widely regarded as being original.[59] In 31:12 it states that the dispersed will come with loud singing to Zion, but with this verse certainty is less about an early date and about Jeremianic authorship. Some think vv 10–14 sound more like the poetry of 2 Isaiah. Volz, who is the main proponent of an early date for the poetry in chapters 30–31, strikes "Zion" in v 12 as a Judaic addition.[60] Bright too believes the passage to be a later "adaptation of Jeremiah's prophecies to the situation of the exiles,"[61] which again calls into question the prophet's support of centralized worship.

---

58. Most recently Norbert Lohfink in "Der junge Jeremia als Propagandist und Poet, Zum Grundstock von Jer 30–31" in *Le Livre de Jérémie* (ed. Pierre-Maurice Bogaert; Leuven: Leuven University, 1981), 351–368.

59. Volz, *Jeremia*, 285–286, comments: "Die Erwähnung des Zion im Mund der Efraimiten könnte auffallen und das Wort ließe sich leicht als Zutat erklären, vgl. 31,12. Doch hat es für die Zeit Jer's nichts Bedenkliches, den Zion als das Zentralheiligtum aller Jahwevereher anzunehmen, weil keine Lokalkulte mehr bestanden vgl. 41,5."

60. Ibid., 280, 286.

61. *Jeremiah*, 286.

The Early Career of the Prophet Jeremiah

There are similar problems with 3:12–13/14. Verse 14 of this passage contains the words, "and I will bring you to Zion," but they come at precisely the point where expansion occurs and scholarly opinion divides over genuineness and the assignment of a date. Some scholars place v 14 with the poetry preceding, others with the prose that follows. The weight of scholarly opinion seems to be against the originality of "Zion" in 14b.[62] And yet there are those who argue that all of 3:12–15 shows Jeremiah as being favorable to centralized worship at Jerusalem.[63]

In 6:16–21 Jeremiah describes his frustration over the people's stubborn refusal to heed his preaching. Verse 16 says:

> Thus says the LORD:
> Stand at the crossroads, and look
>     and ask for the ancient paths
> where the good way lies; and walk in it
>     and find rest for your souls
> But they said, "We will not walk in it."

What are the "ancient paths" Jeremiah has been urging upon the people? Most likely they are Yahweh's torah (v 19). Now if this torah should happen to be Deuteronomy, then Jeremiah is recalling preaching on behalf of the reform. But some think the "ancient paths" refer to Yahweh's *true* torah, i.e., teaching in the spirit of the ancient Sinai covenant (cf. 2:2–3), not from a written code such as Deuteronomy was. The view here is normally held in connection with a particular interpretation of 8:8–9, the passage we will look at next. Those advancing the "true torah" interpretation say that Jeremiah cannot be a proponent of the reform; he has to be a critic, or, at the very least, he must be insisting that the demands of Deuteronomy be tested by ethical principles of a more fundamental sort.[64] Either way, Jeremiah has joined issue with a major reform theme, i.e., obedience to Yahweh's torah/

---

62. Volz, *Jeremia*, 43–44, considers it later eschatology.
63. Lipinski, "Jeremiah" in *EncJud*, 1347.
64. So Skinner, *Prophecy and Religion*, 118.

## An Early Career Beginning before the Reform: The Traditional View

covenant. The passage is therefore given a date in Josiah's reign, usually in the later years.[65]

The brief passage in 8:8–9 has evoked much discussion relative to Deuteronomy and the Josianic Reform. Its authenticity has not been seriously questioned. It reads:

> ⁸How can you say, "We are wise
>   and the law of the LORD is with us"
> when, in fact, the false pen of the scribes
>   has made it into a lie?
> ⁹The wise shall be put to shame
>   they shall be dismayed and taken
> since they have rejected the word of the LORD
>   what wisdom is in them?

Despite uncertainty about the precise meaning of 8b, where an allusion to the reform may occur, the main point of the passage is not in doubt. Certain people are putting on airs, thinking they are wise because they possess the "torah of Yahweh." But this torah in some way has been falsified by the scribes, with the result that those who think they are wise end up rejecting the "word of Yahweh." The basic contrast is then between the "torah of Yahweh" and the "word of Yahweh,"[66] and the "word of Yahweh" in all likelihood is the word Jeremiah is preaching.

Calvin thought this passage was directed against the people as a whole (cf. 5:4–5), but subsequent commentators believe the attack is focused on the priests, who claim the torah (or law) is their possession (18:18). Allied with the priests are the scribes, who in 2:8 are said to be faithless handlers of the torah.

Crucial to interpretation is an identification of the torah which the scribes are falsifying and which is generating among the people a false sense of security. Many suggestions have been made. There seems to be basic agreement that the torah must be a *written* torah because scribes are implicated. Priests deliver also oral torah (cf. 18:18). Luther's translation of 8aß is frequently

---

65. Bright, *Jeremiah*, 50.
66. Rudolph, *Jeremia*, 61; Bright, *Jeremiah*, 63–64.

cited in this connection: "und haben die heilige Schrift vor uns?" Since the written torah must be something less than the whole law, many scholars conclude it is Deuteronomy.[67]

If the torah is Deuteronomy or proto-Deuteronomy, then the controversy fits well into Josiah's reign after 622. The passage is usually not dated after Josiah's death because at that time the nation is thought to be concerned more with political and military matters, not with the reform program.[68] Jeremiah is thus seen to be a critic of Deuteronomy and in opposition to the reform.[69] One should keep also in mind that until not long ago scholars assumed Deuteronomy was authored by priests, which created a splendid opportunity to pit prophet against priest. But the now-prevailing view that Deuteronomy was authored by scribes[70] changes the picture only slightly.

Not everyone, however, is willing to cast Jeremiah as an opponent of the reform. Those who conclude from 11:1-8 and elsewhere that Jeremiah supported the reform, offer different explanations for 8:8-9. Some believe the torah must be a document other than Deuteronomy. It could be what is now called the Priestly Document, which contained regulations about sacrifice.[71] In 7:22-23 Jeremiah is outspokenly critical of temple sacrifice. Another possibility would be a document, now lost, in

---

67. Following the lead of Karl Marti (*Der Prophet Jeremia von Anatot*, 1889), Julius Wellhausen accepted this view in his *Prolegomenon to the History of Ancient Israel* (New York and Cleveland: World Publishing Co., 1957), 403. It was subsequently accepted by Duhm (*Jeremia*, 88), Cornill (*Jeremia*, 116) and others. For additional bibliography see Rowley, "The Early Prophecies of Jeremiah," 232-233.

68. Welch, *Jeremiah: His Time and His Work*, 90.

69. See the works cited in note 66. Welch (ibid., 91-92) argued that the centralization passage of Deut 12:1-7 was a good example of how priests rewrote Deuteronomy.

70. Moshe Weinfeld, "Deuteronomy--The Present State of Inquiry," *JBL* 86 (1967), 249-262; idem, *Deuteronomy and the Deuteronomic School* (Oxford: Clarendon Press, 1972).

71. See discussion in G. A. Smith, *Jeremiah*, 155-156; Bewer, *Jeremiah I*, 35; Rowley, "The Early Prophecies of Jeremiah," 232-233.

## An Early Career Beginning before the Reform: The Traditional View

which priests attempted to regulate pagan worship.[72] Controversial practices such as the ones mentioned in 7:31 and 19:5 give support to this view.

Other scholars conclude that Jeremiah's hostility toward the reform was a later development, and that early on he gave the program his support. When it became clear that the program was shallow, failing to bring people to genuine repentance and giving them instead a false sense of security, Jeremiah became disillusioned, and it is this disillusionment we are hearing in 8:8–9.[73] It is heard also in 6:16–21. Adopting a developmental view scholars are then able to propose a date after Josiah's time for 8:8–9. Bright, for example, prefers a date after 609, though he says the last years of Josiah are also possible. He believes, however, that the passage provides no insight into Jeremiah's original attitude toward the reform and v 8 is not a disparagement of Deuteronomy.[74]

This review has shown that while certain passages in 1–20 and 30–31 appear to reflect reform issues and attitudes which Jeremiah may have had toward the reform, scholarly opinion on a host of other questions—related and unrelated to the reform—bear heavily on how passages get interpreted. Those holding the traditional view bring with them *a priori* assumptions on numerous controversial questions, e.g., the relative merits of prose versus poetry in the book of Jeremiah, the *Weltanschauung* of the true prophet of Yahweh, differences between prophets and priests,[75] how prophets view leaders in politics, government, and

---

72. Giesebrecht, *Jeremia*, 55; Peake, *Jeremiah I*, 160; and Streane, *Jeremiah and Lamentations*, 61. Torrey, "The Background of Jeremiah 1–10," 198, quotes with approval the suggestion by S. R. Driver that pagan practices from the Manasseh period were being enforced.

73. Skinner, *Prophecy and Religion*, 104–106, 119; Rowley, "The Early Prophecies of Jeremiah," 232–234.

74. *Jeremiah*, 63–65.

75. Not everyone contrasted the two offices as sharply as T. J. Meek; see his article, "Was Jeremiah a Priest?" in *The Expositor* 8th Series 25 (1923), 215–222.

## The Early Career of the Prophet Jeremiah

religion—specifically the priesthood[76] and the cult,[77] whether prophets compromise ultimately with programs embodying ideals less lofty than their own,[78] etc. Answers to these questions and others affect to a large degree what conclusions are reached about Jeremiah's relation to the Josianic Reform.

Some believe Jeremiah supported the reform because it shared many of the same principles he stood for.[79] Others say he could not help but recognize how superficial a remedy the reform program was for an illness which went much deeper. Programs institutionally-based are, by their very nature, bound to be concerned more with external changes than with radical changes in the human heart.[80] Some therefore believe that Jeremiah was at no time sympathetic toward the reform.[81]

Another argument used to support the idea that Jeremiah related early in his career to the reform is the close ties known to have existed between the prophet and the scribal family of Shaphan. Shaphan was a key figure in the reform activities of 622 (2 Kings 22), and members of his family gave Jeremiah much-needed protection and other assistance during the difficult years of Jehoiakim, also afterwards (26:24; 29:3; 39:14).[82]

In the final analysis all scholars holding the traditional view posit some relation between Jeremiah and the reform, if only

---

76. Some have argued, for example, that as soon as the newly-discovered lawbook passed into the hands of the priesthood the reform was bound to be neutralized; see e.g., Skinner, *Prophecy and Religion*, 114.

77. On the prophet as a "foe of the cult" see the discussion of H. H. Rowley in "The Prophet Jeremiah and the Book of Deuteronomy," 172–173, and "The Early Prophecies of Jeremiah," 228.

78. Peake, *Jeremiah I*, 13; Skinner, *Prophecy and Religion*, 105–107.

79. Peake, *Jeremiah I*, 12–13; Bewer, *Jeremiah I*, 6; Muilenburg, "Jeremiah the Prophet" in *IDB*, 826.

80. Bright, *Jeremiah*, xciv.

81. Cornill, *Jeremia*, 143–145; Welch, *Jeremiah: His Time and His Work*, 76–96. For additional bibliography see Rowley, "The Early Prophecies of Jeremiah," 228 n.1.

82. Skinner, *Prophecy and Religion*, 107; N. Gottwald, *A Light to the Nations* (New York: Harper & Bros., 1959), 356.

## An Early Career Beginning before the Reform: The Traditional View

because he was active as a prophet while the reform was in progress. His call came before the reform began, and in the traditional view a good bit of preaching was done in the five years prior to 622. It should also be mentioned that some scholars argue for a period of silence during Josiah's later years.[83] But that too has been challenged.[84] Regardless then what precisely Jeremiah was doing between 622 and 609, and how he felt about what was going on in Jerusalem during this time, his early career according to the book's chronology and the traditional view has to be set against the background of the most significant event to take place in Josiah's reign.

## WHO IS THE FOE FROM THE NORTH?

In the early chapters of the book prominence is given to a "foe" which Yahweh announces will be sent by him to wreak mass destruction upon Judah. It will appear out of the north (1:13–15; 4:6; 6:1, 22; 10:22). Jeremiah first hears about this foe in a vision carrying with it a full explanation (1:13–19). Subsequent preaching about the foe is found in the poetry of 4:5–6:30, a unit named for the "foe from the north." Some scholars extend the foe poems all the way into chapter 8.

In 4:5 there is a noticeable change in Jeremiah's preaching. In what preceded, despite much sharp criticism about the nation's idolatry and religious harlotry, an air of social and political calm prevailed. Now there is great agitation, for a military opponent is threatening Jerusalem and its environs. In 4:5–8 Jeremiah is told to announce this threat:

> ⁵Declare in Judah, and proclaim in Jerusalem, and say:
> Blow the trumpet through the land
>  shout aloud and say

---

83. Peake, *Jeremiah I*, 15; G. A. Smith, *Jeremiah*, 132; Muilenburg, "Jeremiah the Prophet" in *IDB*, 826.

84. Bright, *Jeremiah*, lxxxii-lxxxiii, xci-xcvi; see also W. Johnstone, "The Setting of Jeremiah's Prophetic Activity," *TGUOS* 21 (1965–66), 54–55.

## The Early Career of the Prophet Jeremiah

> "Gather together, and let us go
>    into the fortified cities!"
> ⁶Raise a standard toward Zion
>    flee for safety, do not delay
> for I am bringing evil from the north
>    and a great destruction
> ⁷A lion has gone up from its thicket
>    a destroyer of nations has set out
>       he has gone out from his place
> to make your land a waste
>    your cities will be ruins
>    without inhabitant
> ⁸Because of this put on sackcloth
>    lament and wail
> "The fierce anger of the LORD
>    has not turned away from us."

From another passage in 6:22–26 we see that the news terrifies Jeremiah as much as anyone else:

> ²²Thus says the LORD:
> See, a people is coming from the land of the north
>    a great nation is stirring from the farthest parts
>       of the earth
> ²³They grasp the bow and the javelin
>    they are cruel and have no mercy
>       their sound is like the roaring sea
> they ride on horses
>    equipped like a warrior for battle
>    against you, O daughter Zion!
>
> ²⁴"We have heard news of them
>    our hands fall helpless
> anguish has taken hold of us
>    pain as of a woman in labor
> ²⁵Do not go out into the field
>    or walk on the road
> for the enemy has a sword
>    terror is on every side"

## An Early Career Beginning before the Reform: The Traditional View

> ²⁶O my poor people, put on sackcloth
>   and roll in ashes
> make mourning as for an only child
>   most bitter lamentation
> for suddenly the destroyer
>   will come upon us.

Nowhere in these early chapters is the foe identified. Scholars of the pre-critical period (e.g., Calvin) assumed the foe was Babylon, the nation which came finally to end things for Judah.[85] But with modern critical scholarship came a change in thinking about the nature of prophecy, one which forced upon scholars the conclusion that Babylon could not be the foe. Prophets were now said to be "forthtellers," not "foretellers," which is to say the words they spoke had to be anchored in events currently taking place, or, at the very least, in events about to take place shortly. This de-emphasis on predictive prophecy can be seen in Wellhausen and his followers. Since therefore the vision of the foe in 1:13–14 is believed to have come to Jeremiah quite early—indeed many take it as part of the call in 627[86]—and since the preaching about the foe was likewise thought to be some of Jeremiah's earliest preaching between 627 and 622, Babylon at this time is not an imminent foe. Babylon might be perceived as a threat after Nineveh is destroyed in 612,[87] and is surely a threat by 604 when its army is physically present in Palestine,[88] but in 627–622 it poses no threat whatever to Judah.

For scholars in the pre-critical era this was no issue. Prophets can predict events 10–20 years into the future, or 50–100 years. But for critical scholars such an expansive view of predictive

---

85. This pre-critical view is still maintained by conservative scholars such as E. J. Young, *An Introduction to the Old Testament* (Grand Rapids: Wm. B. Eerdmans Publishing Co., 1954), 225.

86. Welch, *Jeremiah: His Time and His Work*, 97; Rowley, "The Early Prophecies of Jeremiah," 206.

87. So Rowley, "The Early Prophecies of Jeremiah," 212–213.

88. Skinner, *Prophecy and Religion*, 42, says Babylon is not a threat until 20 years after Jeremiah's call, i.e., about 606 B.C.

## The Early Career of the Prophet Jeremiah

prophecy is no longer tenable, therefore the gap between prophetic revelation or prophetic announcement on the one hand, and actual happening on the other, has to be narrowed. What is more, a close reading of the poetry in 4:5–6:30 gives the unmistakable impression that a foe is fast approaching the city gates. Many scholars, therefore, holding the traditional view concluded that Babylon could not be the foe from the north.

Who then was the foe? For two centuries or more a long and impressive train of scholars has argued that the foe was likely to be the Scythians, an Indo-Aryan people from southern Russia known to have roamed in hordes during the late Assyrian Age where they caused widespread havoc throughout the empire.[89] The Scythians are attested in the Assyrian texts, and should they be identified also with the Umman-Manda who built Ecbatana and participated in the destruction of Nineveh[90] we have a trace of them all the way down to the beginning of the Persian period.[91] From Herodotus (*History I*, 104–106) we learn that during the time of Psammetichus I of Egypt the Scythians were present in Palestine where they are said to have reigned 28 years. Also, a Scythian presence in Palestine—though not necessarily during

---

89. The view dates from Venema in 1765, according to Cazelles, "Zephaniah, Jeremiah, and the Scythians in Palestine," 145, and was accepted by Eichhorn and Hitzig among others; cf. Rowley, "The Early Prophecies of Jeremiah," 199–200 n. 8. See also Cheyne, *Jeremiah: His Life and Times*, 30–42; Duhm, *Jeremia*, 48; Peake, *Jeremiah I*, 4, 11; Streane, *Jeremiah and Lamentations*, xi-xii; Skinner, *Prophecy and Religion*, 39–44; G. A. Smith, *Jeremiah*, 73, 89, 110–134; Rowley, "The Early Prophecies of Jeremiah," 207, 217; Bewer, *Jeremiah I*, 21; and Muilenburg, "Jeremiah the Prophet" in *IDB*, 825–826.

90. Scholars earlier on made an identification between the Scythians and the Umman-Manda, e.g., Morris Jastrow Jr. in his article, "Babylonia and Assyria" in *EncB* 11th ed., 3, 105; Bright, *Jeremiah*, xliii (though in the 3rd ed. of his *History of Israel*, 315–316, it is not made). Rowley, "The Early Prophecies of Jeremiah," 208, says the Umman-Manda were perhaps an earlier wave of invaders from southern Russia who mingled in finally with the Medes. For further discussion see Cazelles, "Zephaniah, Jeremiah, and the Scythians in Palestine," 138–144.

91. Jastrow, ibid.

## An Early Career Beginning before the Reform: The Traditional View

the years we are now concerned with—is evidenced by other historical and archaeological data.[92]

The testimony of Herodotus, however, has been widely questioned. Even those who hold the "Scythian hypothesis" concede that he exaggerates and is sometimes unreliable.[93] Some discount him out of hand. Nevertheless, the Scythian hypothesis has attracted a large number of adherents. Duhm popularized the hypothesis by calling the poems in 4:5–6:30 the "Scythian Songs." Among those rejecting the hypothesis are some who interpret the foe eschatologically.[94] But the majority of scholars agree with Wellhausen that the foe has to be a concrete historical enemy in the pre-exilic period.[95]

Identifying the foe still presents a problem for the traditional view, since scholars by and large have backed away from the Scythian hypothesis or abandoned it altogether. Bright, the historian, recognizes that the Scythians were active during the late Assyrian Age, but he remains tentative with respect to the testimony of Herodotus.[96] Form criticism comes to his aid at this point by enabling him to disassociate the vision of the foe

---

92. Bethshan was known in the Greek period as Scythopolis; see Rowley, "The Early Prophecies of Jeremiah," 210; also R. W. Hamilton, "Beth-shan" in *IDB* A-D, 397–401.

93. Skinner, *Prophecy and Religion*, 39; and Rowley, "The Early Prophecies of Jeremiah," 208–212, who, however, does not dismiss him out of hand.

94. Rowley, "The Early Prophecies of Jeremiah," 207, who cites the original work of Fritz Wilke, "Das Skythenproblem im Jeremiabuch" in *Alttestamentliche Studien*, BWAT 13 (Leipzig: J. C. Hinrichs'sche Buchhandlung, 1913), 222–254. See also Volz, *Jeremia*, 50–51; Welch, *Jeremiah: His Time and His Work*, 97–131; and Torrey, "The Background of Jeremiah 1–10," 208.

95. See Brevard S. Childs, "The Enemy from the North and the Chaos Tradition," *JBL* 78 (1959), 187–198 [=Perdue and Kovacs 1984: 151–161].

96. Bright, *A History of Israel*, 315; idem, *Jeremiah*, lxxx-lxxxii. Cazelles, "Zephaniah, Jeremiah, and the Scythians in Palestine," 149, is more positive about the testimony of Herodotus. He concludes "that there was a 'Scythian domination' in Syro-Palestine, but it had only been a last reflection of Assyrian control."

from the call in chapter 1,[97] and to date the foe poems later.[98] Weiser, Rudolph, and Berridge are back to identifying the foe with Babylon.[99]

Part of the problem has to do with descriptions given of the foe in 1:13–15 and 4:5–6:30. The "tribes of the kingdoms of the north" in 1:15 could be roving bands such as the Scythians were,[100] but they might also be a coalition force such as the one which attacked Nineveh in 612. In 5:15 the foe is described as follows:

> I am going to bring upon you
>    a nation from far away, O house of Israel
>      says the LORD
> It is an enduring nation
>    it is an ancient nation[101]
> a nation whose language you do not know
>    nor can you understand what they say.

The Babylonians spoke an alien language, but so did the Indo-Aryan Scythians. The mention of a "nation" (Heb *gôy*)—particularly an enduring and ancient nation—makes the foe sound more like Babylon. In 6:22–26 a mighty foe is again depicted, a "great nation" complete with bows, spears, and cavalry. This fits Babylon better than some loosely organized band of raiders. Usually when all the foe poems are analyzed it is concluded that all could easily describe the Babylonians, but not all could fit the Scythians. Therefore some holding the Scythian hypothesis propose that the foe poems were spoken originally in the face of a Scythian threat, then "touched up" later so as to apply to the Babylonians.[102]

    97. *Jeremiah*, 6–8.

    98. Ibid., xcvi.

    99. Weiser, *Jeremia*, 43–44; Rudolph, *Jeremia*, 48–49; Berridge, *Prophet, People, and the Word of Yahweh*, 76–88.

    100. Rowley, "The Early Prophecies of Jeremiah," 214.

    101. The line, "It is an enduring nation, it is an ancient nation" is lacking in the LXX.

    102. Muilenburg, "Jeremiah the Prophet" in *IDB*, 826; Rowley, "The Early Prophecies of Jeremiah," 218–220. Rowley, however, says there is no proof

## An Early Career Beginning before the Reform: The Traditional View

Those who hold the Scythian hypothesis usually go on to say that nothing much came of the threat, and as a result Jeremiah's predictions went unfulfilled. This could have contributed to his disillusionment and made necessary a period of inactivity for the prophet, which is what many holding the traditional view suppose.[103]

In one other passage Jeremiah refers to warnings he had issued about impending war. It is 6:17, and follows the summons we looked at earlier to return to the "ancient paths". It reads:

> Also I raised up sentinels for you:
> "Give heed to the sound of the trumpet!"
> But they said, "We will not give heed."

The people it seems were no more receptive to Jeremiah's war preaching than to his preaching on behalf of the reform. A date for 6:16–21, as we mentioned earlier, is usually assigned to the final years of Josiah's reign.

Here in 6:16–21 we may have a clue to the two main thrusts in Jeremiah's early preaching. First, there was a reform message basically, a summons for people to return to the "ancient paths". This would translate into obedient living according to standards set forth in the ancient Mosaic covenant, possibly even the revised and updated version known as Deuteronomy. It would also translate into a repudiation of idolatry and religious harlotry. Then came a message about war which would come upon Judah via a foe from the north. The people heeded neither message, and as a result the nation fell.

In spite of all the evidence amassed to support an early career during the reign of Josiah—gathered in large part from undated material—there are those who dismiss it and argue that the chronology supporting the traditional view has to be questioned. To these challenges we now turn.

---

either way. Bright, *Jeremiah*, 50, agrees.

103. Peake, *Jeremiah I*, 11; Rowley, "The Early Prophecies of Jeremiah," 200, 218.

# 2

# A Career Beginning after the Reform: Challenges to the Traditional View

## EARLY ATTEMPTS AT A LOW CHRONOLOGY

OVER A PERIOD OF years a dedicated group of scholars has challenged the most basic assumption undergirding the traditional view, i.e., that the stated chronology in the book can be relied upon. As we have just seen, chronology is the linchpin holding the traditional view intact. These scholars, however, say that the accepted chronology cannot be correct and Jeremiah's dates must in some way be revised downward.

All the problems cited in connection with mapping out a career using the traditional dates are brought forward as argument. It is said, for example, that nothing from Jeremiah can be assurredly assigned to the reign of Josiah. The poetry in chapters 1–20 and 30–31 is of course undated. As for the superscription in 3:6, which mentions the "days of King Josiah," it is said to be late and unreliable. The reason: The passage introduced about the two adulterous sisters is (late) prose and post-dates Ezekiel 16 and 23. The call for covenant obedience in 11:1–17 is also late prose, if not from Jehoiakim's reign, then dating from the exilic or post-exilic periods. As for 2:14–19, despite the reference to Assyria, a date after 609 must be assigned because v 16 looks *back* on the Battle of Megiddo (609 B.C.). It has also been suggested that "Assyria" refers to "Babylon" as it does in some later sources (cf. Zech 10:10–11).

Reference is commonly made to the embarrassing silence in all of our sources about some relationship between Jeremiah and Josiah, or between Jeremiah and the reform program. The mention in 2 Chr 35:25 of Jeremiah giving a lament at Josiah's funeral can be discounted because the Chronicler is late and unreliable. Besides, already in 609 Josiah's reign is ended. Since also many who follow the high chronology propose a "silent period" after 622, it seems preferable to the challengers to begin Jeremiah's career after the reform is over, which is when the dated prose in the book picks up on his activities.

The challenge is strongest, however, at the point where the Scythians are said to be the "foe from the north." These scholars reject the Scythian hypothesis and say that the foe has to be Babylon. Here a lower chronology is crucial, for without it one is back to the pre-critical notion of Jeremiah announcing a foe 10–20 years in advance of its coming. By the time Jehoiakim is king, Babylon is an "imminent" foe.

A lower chronology thus eliminates or seriously curtails a ministry for Jeremiah in the reign of Josiah; there is little or no preaching in the late Assyrian Age, little or no ministry in relation to the reform, and Babylon is back to being the foe from the north. Most important perhaps of all, the call of the prophet is now dated subsequent to 627.

As early as 1895 H. Winckler expressed doubts about the dates in 1:2 and 25:3, concluding that Jeremiah's ministry began around 610.[1] In 1921 Karl Budde raised similar questions about the reliability of the book's chronology, stressing the late date of 1:1–2 and commenting upon the awkwardness of the Hebrew in

---

1. Hugo Winckler, *Geschichte Israels I* (Leipzig: Verlag von Eduard Pfeiffer, 1895), 112–113.

the superscription.² He argued further that the LXX of 1:1, which differs from the MT, could well presuppose a Hebrew superscription which at one time was shorter than the present one and more comparable to the superscriptions in Hosea, Joel, Micah and Zephaniah. This could eliminate the reference to the 13th year of Josiah. At a later time additional information was added, so the argument runs, but because of its lateness doubts may be raised about its historical value. The same basic argument is used with regard to the superscriptions of certain psalms.

In 1923 F. Horst discussed the matter of chronology in a long journal article³ in which he came to the conclusion that Jeremiah's call followed Josiah's death in 609. Along with Budde he rejected 1:2 as late editorializing, and the dates in 25:3; 3:6 and 36:2 were judged to be secondary, and therefore eliminated. Horst said:

> The prevailing chronology, in which the public appearance of Jeremiah is established at 626, is historically false; it is based on an artificial and biased tradition, moreover one which is secondary. An original tradition located rather his public appearance immediately after the Battle of Megiddo.⁴

For Horst Jeremiah's career begins in 609 or shortly thereafter, corresponding to the accession of Jehoiakim to the throne.

In 1932 T. C. Gordon came up with a lower chronology by proposing that the number "thirteen" in 1:2 was a scribal mistake for the number "twenty-three."⁵ Such a mistake could be the result of only one or two minor changes in the Hebrew. This put the call at 616, which, according to the then newly-published Babylonian Chronicle, was the year the siege on Nineveh began. Gordon said nothing about the dates in 25:3; 3:6 and 36:2, but he

---

2. Karl Budde, "Über das erste Kapitel des Buches Jeremia," *JBL* 40 (1921), 23-37.

3. F. Horst, "Die Anfänge des Propheten Jeremia," *ZAW* 41 (1923), 94-153.

4. Ibid., 132.

5. T. C. Gordon, "A New Date for Jeremiah," *ET* 44 (1932-33), 562-565.

was thorough enough in recounting all the standard arguments against the traditional view.

Hans Bardtke in 1935 followed Gordon's line of reasoning, and was able to cite J. Lewy in support of the idea that "thirteen" and "twenty-three" owe their confusion to 25:3 where both numbers occur.[6] He agreed that Jeremiah's call must be seen against the backdrop of Babylon's rise to power, and suggested for Jeremiah's birth a date around 635–634 B.C.

## THE LOW CHRONOLOGIES OF J. PHILIP HYATT

The proposals of text corruption by Gordon and Bardtke went nowhere, and were quickly forgotton. They were rejected by J. Philip Hyatt, the next person of note to take up the banner for a low chronology. Hyatt, however, kept alive the idea that the beginning of Jeremiah's career must be charted against the backdrop of Babylonian ascendancy. Beginning with an article in 1940[7] Hyatt agreed with Horst that 1:2 was unreliable and that the dates in 25:3; 3:6 and 36:2 were secondary. These, said Hyatt, were "the product of a late tradition which sought to show that Jeremiah must have begun his career before the Deuteronomic reforms and that he approved of those reforms."[8] Hyatt therefore proceeded to determine a date for Jeremiah's call and the beginning of his career by correlating events related in the Babylonian Chronicle with details gleaned from the foe poems. His conclusion was that the career began between 614–612 B.C. Support for his position came a few years later from H. G. May.[9]

---

6. Hans Bardtke, "Jeremia der Fremdvölkerprophet," *ZAW* 53 (1935), 218–220.

7. J. Philip Hyatt, "The Peril from the North in Jeremiah," *JBL* 59 (1940), 499–513.

8. Ibid., 513.

9. Herbert G. May, "The Chronology of Jeremiah's Oracles," *JNES* 4 (1945), 217–227.

Publications during the next decade or so affirmed the same basic view, and reiterated the position taken initially that nowhere in the book was there any indication that Jeremiah supported Josiah's reform.[10] Hyatt, however, was uncomfortable with Jeremiah's reported ties with the Shaphan family (26:24; 29:3; 36:10–12; 39:14; etc.; cf. 2 Kgs 22:3–14). He therefore offered the explanation that the Shaphan mentioned in 2 Kgs 22:12, who had a son Ahikam referred to in Jer 26:24 and 39:14, was not Shaphan the scribe mentioned four verses earlier in 2 Kgs 22:8.[11]

When Hyatt's commentary on Jeremiah appeared in the *Interpreter's Bible* in 1956, the view that 1:2 was late and unreliable had been abandoned.[12] It was now believed that the superscription had been authored by Jeremiah's scribal associate Baruch, and that the superscription at one time had served to introduce Baruch's memoirs. The reference to the 13th year of Josiah was thus authentic, but it was not to be taken as the beginning of Jeremiah's career; instead it marked the date of Jeremiah's *birth*. Baruch, Hyatt surmised, could be expected to know Jeremiah's birth date because he was a close friend. The call passage in 1:4–10 was also judged by Hyatt to issue from Baruch's hands, and the linkage Baruch intended from v 2 was not to v 4, as was commonly assumed, but to v 5 where it stated that Jeremiah was "chosen and consecrated to be a prophet even within his mother's womb."[13] This new proposal lowered the chronology another five years. The call and the beginning of the career were now dated ca. 609/8 at which time Jeremiah was 17 or 18 years old. Hyatt's chronology was thus brought into line with the chronology of Horst.

---

10. Hyatt, "Torah in the Book of Jeremiah," *JBL* 60 (1941), 381–396; "Jeremiah and Deuteronomy," *JNES* 1 (1942), 156–173 [=Perdue and Kovacs 1984: 113–127]; "Jeremiah and War," *Crozer Quarterly* 20 (1943), 52–58; and "The Deuteronomic Edition of Jeremiah," *Vanderbilt Studies in the Humanities* 1 (1951), 71–95 [=Perdue and Kovacs 1984: 247–267].

11. "Jeremiah and Deuteronomy," 166.

12. "Jeremiah" in *IB* 5, 797–798.

13. Ibid., 798.

This newer view was restated a decade later[14] when Hyatt responded to another proposal for a low chronology made by C. F. Whitley.[15] Whitley had argued that the career should begin in 605 since that is the first precise chronology in the book (25:1: "the 4th year of Jehoiakim"). Hyatt refuted that idea, but he did agree with Whitley that Jeremiah's temple sermon (7; 26) was his first important public utterance. Whitley thought Jeremiah was a stranger when he appeared before the people on that occasion and then made to stand trial.[16]

## THE LOW CHRONOLOGIES OF WILLIAM L. HOLLADAY

Hyatt's low chronology was widely rejected in the 1960s, e.g., by Muilenburg, Rowley, Bright, Rudolph, and others, but it did not die. William Holladay took it up in an article of 1964,[17] and reasserted it in subsequent publications. Like Hyatt, Holladay has had two views of Jeremiah's career, the second but a slightly modified version of the first. The second view appeared initially in the article, "The Years of Jeremiah's Preaching" (1983),[18] and is repeated in Holladay's *Jeremiah 1* commentary for Hermeneia.[19] Both views, however, adhere to just one chronology, which is Hyatt's second based on the interpretation of 1:2 as the year of Jeremiah's birth.

Holladay approaches the study of Jeremiah's career from a different angle. He first mounts a quest for the prophet's "self

---

14. Hyatt, "The Beginning of Jeremiah's Prophecy," *ZAW* 78 (1966), 204–214 [= Perdue and Kovacs 1984: 63–72].

15. C. F. Whitley, "The Date of Jeremiah's Call," *VT* 14 (1964), 467–483 [= Perdue and Kovacs 1984: 73–87].

16. Ibid., 469.

17. W. L. Holladay, "The Background of Jeremiah's Self-Understanding: Moses, Samuel, and Psalm 22," *JBL* 83 (1964), 153–164 [= Perdue and Kovacs 1984: 313–324].

18. See chapter 1 note 4.

19. See "A Chronology of Jeremiah's Career," 1–10, which summarizes the views of earlier articles.

understanding," which leads him to analyze vocabulary and phrasaeology of selected passages, also distinctive modes of thought. What he discovers is that Jeremiah from an early age was conscious of living out his life against the background of two larger-than-life prophets from Israel's past: Moses and Samuel.[20]

A connection with Moses has long been noted. Jerome, as we mentioned earlier, compared and contrasted the call passage of 1:4–10 with Moses' call in Exodus 3–4. But Holladay brings into active discussion Deut 18:18, a passage occasionally cited by commentators[21] but seldom discussed in connection with Jeremiah's call because Deuteronomy is thought to be unavailable in 627, becoming public only in 622. It is the same problem discussed earlier when the question was whether Deut 24:1–4 might have influenced Jer 3:1. One way around the problem here would be to argue that Deut 18:18 did influence the call, but the influence which came was subequent to 622 when Jeremiah put his experience into words. This was the explanation offered by Muilenburg.[22]

Holladay's low chronology, however, is another solution. Deut 18:18 is important for Holladay if Jeremiah is thinking of himself as the "prophet like Moses." In it Yahweh addresses Moses saying:

> I will raise up for them a prophet like you from
> among their brethern; and *I will put my words
> in his mouth, and he shall speak* to them *all that
> I command him.*
> (Deut 18:18 RSV)

The verbal parallels to Jeremiah's call are unmistakable:

> ... *and all that I command you you shall speak*
> (Jer 1:7 Mine)

20. Holladay, "The Background of Jeremiah's Self-Understanding."

21. Peake, *Jeremiah I*, 7; Streane, *Jeremiah and Lamentations*, 3; Welch, *Jeremiah: His Time and His Work*, 88, where the citation is to Deut 18:15; and Bewer, *Jeremiah I*, 12.

22. "Jeremiah the Prophet" in *IDB*, 825.

> Then the LORD put forth his hand and touched
> my mouth; and the LORD said to me, "Behold,
> *I have put my words in your mouth* . . .
> (Jer 1:9 RSV)

According to Holladay Jeremiah receives the call in 609 when he is 17 years old. Josiah has just been killed, and it is imagined that Jeremiah had an experience similar to Isaiah's when Yahweh called him, i.e., "in the year that King Uzziah died" (Isa 6:1). In this critical moment of Judah's history Jeremiah understands himself to be the prophet of Deut 18:18. The reform is over, and no one else is available to step forward. The new King Jehoiakim, says Holladay, "was certainly no devotee of Moses."[23]

Holladay finds that traditions about Samuel also impact Jeremiah's self-understanding. This supports his interpretation of 1:2 to the extent that Samuel was also set aside for prophetic office from birth.[24]

A follow-up article[25] strengthens the "prophet like Moses" thesis. Two lines of reasoning are pursued. In the first Holladay shows that vocabulary and phraseology in the early Jeremianic poetry—particularly in chapter 2—closely parallel vocabulary and phraseology found in the Song of Moses (Deuteronomy 32). This discovery was not new,[26] but Holladay's conclusion was, that the Song provided Jeremiah with diction for his earliest preaching. Holladay even wondered whether the Song might not be part of the 622 lawbook. If so, there is added reason to want a low chronology because the Song would not have been available between 627 and 622, the years which, according to the traditional view, Jeremiah was preaching the oracles of chapter 2.

The low chronology also made possible a new interpretation for 15:16. Accepting a suggestion which I made to him, Holladay

---

23. "The Background of Jeremiah's Self-Understanding," 162.
24. Ibid.
25. "Jeremiah and Moses: Further Observations," *JBL* 85 (1966), 17–27.
26. It was noticed by a number of the older commentators, e.g., Henderson, *Jeremiah and Lamentations*, 7–9, 20; Cheyne, *Jeremiah: His Life and Times*, 25, 84; and Streane, *Jeremiah and Lamentations*, 10.

argued that the phrase, "your words were found" (Heb *nimṣĕ'û dĕbāreykā*), which begins this verse, reflects not upon the call but upon the finding of the lawbook in the temple.[27] In 2 Kgs 22:13 Josiah makes reference to "the *words* of this book that has been found" (Heb *dibrê hassēper hannimĕṣā' hazzeh*). According to the usual interpretation the "words" in 15:16—which are Yahweh's words—came to Jeremiah in the call, for the verse continues, "and I ate them." The image coming immediately to mind is that of Ezekiel eating the scroll containing Yahweh's words at the time he was called (Ezek 2:8–3:3). But the verb "find" (Heb *māṣā'*) is unusual; we should rather expect *hāyāh* (1:4, 11, 13; *et passim*). Yet if he is recalling the finding of the lawbook, *māṣā'* is precisely the word he would use.

Holladay correctly notes that this interpretation has probably not been considered before because of the chronological problems arising in connection with the traditional view. The flow of thought requires that the "finding" come before the "eating," and if the eating takes place in 627, the finding cannot be five years later in 622. But with a low chronology the problem is eliminated. Jeremiah first alludes to the finding of the lawbook, then 13 years later, when the call is received (in 609), the words on the scroll are consumed. Jeremiah in this act puts himself forward as the prophet like Moses.

These new ideas along with certain others are placed in a wider context in Holladay's more popular book, *Jeremiah: Spokesman Out of Time*, published in 1974.[28] The final defense of his first view on the career is made in an article of 1981 in which things remain basically unchanged.[29] Passages used to support the traditional view are discussed in more detail and some new

---

27. "Jeremiah and Moses: Further Observations," 23. I have never, however, subscribed to Holladay's low chronology; see my article, "The Lawbook of the Josianic Reform," 302, and the discussion following.

28. (Philadelphia: Pilgrim Press, 1974).

29. "A Coherent Chronology of Jeremiah's Early Career" in P.-M. Bogaert, *Le Livre de Jérémie*, 58–73.

arguments are made in support of the low chronology. These derive from dates assigned to passages which are thought to be included on the early scrolls mentioned in Jeremiah 36.[30]

In his 1983 article, "The Years of Jeremiah's Preaching," Holladay retains the notion that 627 is the year of Jeremiah's birth, but the call and the beginning of the career are pushed back into the last years of Josiah. Holladay has now become persuaded by Lohfink[31] that chapters 30-31 contain preaching by the young Jeremiah on behalf of Josiah's program to bring about religious and political union of north and south. This is the program set forth in 2 Kgs 23:15-18/20. Holladay finds more early preaching towards the north in 2:1-4:4, though in its present context it dates from a later time.[32] At any rate, Jeremiah is now said to be active *before* the Battle of Megiddo, which means an abandonment of the correlation made earlier between the call and the traumatic events of 609.

Now Holladay must find a new date for the call and the beginning of the career. He does this by first developing a scheme for the public reading of Deuteronomy. According to Deut 31:9-13 the law was to be read at the Feast of Booths at seven-year intervals. Assuming Deuteronomy was read at Booths in the celebration year of 622, Holladay imagines subsequent public readings every seven years thereafter. The next observance of Booths would be in 615, and this is the year now chosen as the one in which Jeremiah received his call. It is further assumed by Holladay that Jeremiah uses the occasion of Deuteronomy's seven-year readings to issue "counter-proclamations." Following the announcement of his call in 615, there would be counter-proclamations in 608, 601, 594, and 587 B.C. In 601, for example,

---

30. Holladay, "The Identification of the Two Scrolls of Jeremiah," *VT* 30 (1980), 452-467; see also *idem, The Architecture of Jeremiah 1-20* (Lewisburg: Bucknell University Press, 1976)

31. Norbert Lohfink,"Der junge Jeremia als Propagandist und Poet, Zum Grundstock von Jer 30-31."

32. "The Years of Jeremiah's Preaching," 148.

a counter-proclamation is made on the drought (8:4–13);[33] in 594 one on covenant obedience (11:1–16);[34] etc. At this point in the reconstruction Holladay's many interrelated assumptions have long since outrun the evidence, and the reasoning is purely circular. Details of the scheme also remain unclear.

Perhaps the most far-reaching implication of this second view of the career is that Jeremiah is only 12 years old when the call comes. Holladay points out, however, that at 12 Jesus was discoursing with teachers in the temple. Yet the assumption here is a much larger one: At the age of 12 or sometime after—Holladay is not clear—Jeremiah embarks on a public career and is preaching in support of Josiah's centralization program.[35]

The low chronologies of Hyatt and Holladay do have a certain appeal. With the Scythian hypothesis now widely abandoned and the foe agreed to be Babylon, we very much need to compress the time between the vision of the foe and the preaching about the foe on one hand, and Babylon's arrival in Palestine on the other. Yet by placing the call and the beginning of the career at 609, or even 615, the time frame for the career is compressed too much. Hyatt makes the remark that the seven-year period following the reading of the first scroll (i.e., 604–598) was "one of the busiest in the life of the prophet, though he must have been in hiding for part of the time."[36] The proviso alone is reason enough to give us pause before accepting this statement (cf. 36:19, 26). The statement itself rings hollow if the prose tradition in the book is to believed. The only dated prose which can possibly fit in between 604 and 598 is chapter 35, and its date is disputed, which means Hyatt is assuming at least as much about all the undated material as those holding the traditional view, who suggest that the bulk of it comes from the reign of Josiah. Holladay runs into the same problem. He ends up dating an inordinate amount of

---

33. *Jeremiah I*, 277.
34. Ibid., 351.
35. Ibid., 2.
36. "Jeremiah" in *IB*, 780.

material in chapters 1–25 to 601–600 B.C., years which according to the prose tradition Jeremiah's ministry was curtailed if not suspended entirely.[37]

On the positive side, however, it must be recognized that Holladay's work has made possible an expanded discussion of the career and new interpretations for specific Jeremianic texts. Deut 18:18 certainly appears to be an influence on Jeremiah's call in 1:4–10; Deut 24:1–4 is clearly background for the argument in 3:1; and Deuteronomy 32 impacts the poetry of chapter 2 without question. Also, the new interpretation for 15:16a ("your words were found") reads the Hebrew better, and for the first time identifies a clear reference in the book to the events of 622, about which we have long expected there to be at least some mention.

But Holladay's second view of the call and career beginning has a problem so far as Jeremiah's age is concerned. He is simply too young. Jerome took the position that Jeremiah began prophesying while he was still a "boy" (*puer*), but Calvin—who also called Jeremiah a *puer*—dismissed the idea as frivolous,[38] and to my knowledge no one has seriously made such a proposal since, that is until Holladay has come up now with a date of 615 for the call and an age for Jeremiah of 12 years at the time. Jeremiah cannot begin his career at 12 years of age. One may even question whether at 18 he can be delivering the important temple oracles of 609, which caused such a sensation and brought about a major trial.[39]

The root problem with both Hyatt and Holladay's attempts at a low chronology is Hyatt's interpretation of 1:2, which Holladay accepts. This verse cannot mean what they say it does, viz., that "the 13th year of Josiah" is the year of Jeremiah's birth. In the first place, it would be unlikely in the extreme for Baruch—or any other scribe—to speak so cryptically in a superscription where straight talk is the rule. In poetry, yes, but not in a superscription

---

37. See Holladay, *Jeremiah I*.
38. Calvin, *Jeremiah and Lamentations I*, 31.
39. Holladay, *Jeremiah I*, 2–3.

or other statement giving chronology. The genre does not admit this sort of thing.[40]

Secondly, Hyatt and Holladay build their connection on a reading of 1:5 which cannot be sustained. In 1:5 the accent is not on Jeremiah's birth, but on *a time preceding* birth and conception. Yahweh says he knew, consecrated, and appointed Jeremiah *before* he was formed in the womb, *before* he was born. Twice the Hebrew has *bĕṭerem*, "before". One cannot therefore derive from 1:5 the idea that Jeremiah was called from birth. The statement here is hyperbole and as such carries with it no specificity whatsoever; in fact the entire thrust of Yahweh's words is to rule out specificity. The call comes not in the present moment when Yahweh is speaking to Jeremiah; nor did it come when Jeremiah lay hidden in his mother's womb; it was issued *before*—at a time known only to Yahweh.

Thirdly, the thought link between the superscription and the call, which is created editorially, comes in the wording of 1:2 and 1:4 as scholars have long noted. In 1:2 it says regarding Jeremiah that "the word of the LORD *came* to him" (*hāyāh dĕbar-yhwh 'ēlāyw*) in the 13th year of Josiah; in 1:4 Jeremiah himself says, "and the word of the LORD *came* to me:" (*wayĕhî dĕbar-yhwh 'ēlāy*), after which the dialogue of the call follows. Between 1:2 and 1:5 there is no thought link at all.

It is not surprising then that the low chronologies of Hyatt and Holladay have failed to win acceptance. Besides being rejected by virtually every commentator in the past four decades who stays with the traditional view, they are rejected by Thiel who inclines to an early career in Josiah's reign on the basis of 36:2, and by McKane and Herrmann who favor the argument for a low chronology proposed by Horst.[41] One recent author is

---

40. See the comments of Thiel, *Die deuteronomistische Redaktion von Jeremia 1–25*, 61; and Herrmann, *Jeremia: Der Prophet und Das Buch*, 6.

41. Thiel, ibid., 60–61; McKane, *Jeremiah I*, 3–5; Herrmann, ibid., 6, 30.

*A Career Beginning after the Reform: Challenges to the Traditional View*

found leaning toward a date of 627 for Jeremiah's birth, but no credit is given to either Hyatt or Holladay.[42]

---

42. Michael Grant, *The History of Ancient Israel* (New York: Charles Scribner's Sons, 1984), 154.

# 3

# An Early Career Beginning at the Height of the Reform: A New View

## THE CALL TO BE A PROPHET (1:4-12)

WHAT NEEDS TO BE challenged is not the chronology in the book, which is clear, consistent, and gives every indication of being secure. It is rather the idea that Jeremiah's call and the beginning of his career take place simultaneously, or if not simultaneously at least very nearly so. This unexamined assumption virtually everyone makes—whether they hold the traditional view or challenge that view with a lower chronology.

For scholars holding the traditional view this assumption raises too high Jeremiah's age when he is called. Also, a date of 627 B.C. for the vision of the foe—which derives additionally from a unified view of chapter 1—is too early and precludes an identification of the foe with Babylon. Bracketing out both visions, as Duhm and Mowinckel do, creates exegetical and interpretive problems of a different sort, as we shall see in a moment. Dates between 627 and 622 for Jeremiah's earliest preaching—particularly the foe poems—are the primary reason for a poor correlation between material in chapters 1–20 and known events during Josiah's reign. Jerome and Holladay, on the other hand, bring down too low Jeremiah's age for the beginning of a public career. Also, Holladay's correlation of material in chapters 1–20 with events during Jehoiakim's reign is a partial success only because of the confessions in 11–20.

The vision of the foe and the beginning of Jeremiah's career must both be dated later than 627—some years later—if the traditional view is to be relieved of the strain it is under, and selected passages in chapters 1–20 are to find reasonable correlation with events during Josiah's reign. The problematic chapter is the first one in the book, to which we now turn.

The passage of call and commission in 1:4–19 reads:

> [4] Now the word of the LORD came to me saying,
> [5] "Before I formed you in the
>   womb I knew you
> and before you were born I
>   consecrated you
> I appointed you a prophet to
>   the nations"
> [6] Then I said, "Ah, Lord God! Truly I do not know how to speak, for I am only a boy." [7] But the LORD said to me,
>   "Do not say, 'I am only a boy'
>   for you shall go to all to whom I send you
>   and you shall speak whatever I command you
> [8] Do not be afraid of them
>   for I am with you to deliver you
>     says the LORD."
> [9] Then the LORD put out his hand and touched my mouth; and the LORD said to me,
>   "Now I have put my words in your mouth
> [10] See, today I appoint you over nations and over kingdoms
>   to pluck up and to pull down
>   to destroy and to overthrow
>   to build and to plant."
> [11] The word of the LORD came to me, saying, "Jeremiah, what do you see?" And I said, "I see a branch of an

almond tree." ¹²Then the LORD said to me, "You have seen well, for I am watching over my word to perform it."

¹³The word of the LORD came to me a second time, saying, "What do you see?" And I said, "I see a boiling pot, tilted away from the north." ¹⁴Then the LORD said to me: Out of the north disaster shall break out on all the inhabitants of the land.

¹⁵For now I am calling all the tribes of the kingdoms of the north, says the LORD; and they shall come and all of them shall set their thrones at the entrance of the gates of Jerusalem, against all its surrounding walls and against all the cities of Judah. ¹⁶And I will utter my judgments against them, for all their wickedness in forsaking me; they have made offerings to other gods, and worshiped the works of their own hands. ¹⁷But you, gird up your loins; stand up and tell them everything that I command you. Do not break down before them, or I will break you before them. ¹⁸And I for my part have made you today a fortified city, an iron pillar, and a bronze wall, against the whole land—against the kings of Judah, its princes, its priests, and the people of the land. ¹⁹They will fight against you; but they shall not prevail against you, for I am with you, says the LORD, to deliver you.

There are problems with Duhm and Mowinckel's view that the two visions, said to comprise vv 11–16, be bracketed out.[1] Looking at the superscriptions in 1:2, 4, 11, 13 and 2:1, as well as superscriptions of a similar nature in other parts of the book, it is by no means obvious that v 11 signals a new beginning. In fact, this superscription is better understood as a repetition of the superscriptions in vv 2 and 4. The superscription in v 13 makes the new beginning. It says, "and the word of the LORD came to me *a second time* (Heb *šēnît*)."[2] Were the new beginning at v 11, this superscription in v 13—in the final composition, at least—would

---

1. Duhm, *Jeremia*, 10–11; Mowinckel, *Zur Komposition des Buches Jeremia*, 20.
2. Lundbom, "Rhetorical Structures in Jeremiah 1," *ZAW* 103 (1991), 201–203.

## An Early Career Beginning at the Height of the Reform: A New View

have to say "third," not "second" (the first word coming in v 4, the second in v 11, and the third in v 13).[3] The division comes between vv 12 and 13, which is to say the vision of the almond rod belongs to the experience of call.

There is no break at all after v 16. A rhetorical structure beginning at v 15 concludes with either v 18 or v 19.[4] It is as follows in outline form:

> [15]*Look, I* am calling all the tribes of the north . . .
>     (to) Jerusalem . . .
> against all its *walls* round about
>     and against all the *cities* of Judah . . .
>
> [17]*But you* (Jeremiah), get dressed, go out and speak
>     to (Jerusalem) . . .
>
> [18]*And I, look* I have made you today
>     into a fortified *city* . . .
> and into *walls* of bronze against all the land . . .

Key words contrast the divine "I" and "you" (Jeremiah), and include a repetition of *hinnê*. The sequence of v 18 inverts the sequence of v 15: "Look, I . . . I, look." Verses 15 and 18 contain another chiasmus in "walls . . . cities . . . city . . . walls." These repetitions—with inversion—highlight the main point of Yahweh's speech, i.e., that Jerusalem's walls and Judah's cities will fall to the foe from the north, but Jeremiah, with divine protection rendering him a virtual fortified city and walls of bronze, will have his salvation assured.

The whole of chapter 1, in fact, has a rhetorical structure as I have pointed out before:

> A  Articulation of the call (4–10)
>   B  Vision of the call (11–12)
>   B'  Vision of the commission (13–14)
> A'  Articulation of the commission (15–19)

---

3. This is noted by Bright, *Jeremiah*, 7–8, and also by Berridge, *Prophet, People, and the Word of Yahweh*, 67.

4. Lundbom, "Rhetorical Structures in Jeremiah 1," 204–205; see earlier my *Jeremiah: A Study in Ancient Hebrew Rhetoric*, 96–99 (1997: 127–130).

## The Early Career of the Prophet Jeremiah

The chapter reports two experiences in the life of Jeremiah: 1) a call from Yahweh (1:4–12); and 2) a commission to begin a public ministry (1:13–19). The first vision of the almond rod belongs with the call; the second vision of the pot spilling over from the north belongs with the commissioning. There are two visions, two divine words, and two experiences in the life of the prophet. By design the visions have been placed in the center. The sequence in the commission narrative is the one we are accustomed to seeing—where the vision comes first and the expanded articulation second. See, e.g., 24:1–10, and with variation, Amos 7:1–9. But in the call narrative the expanded articulation comes first and the vision second, making a chiasmus for the whole.

The call then continues to be dated to 627 B.C., but the commission comes later. How much later the text does not say. In a moment we will be in a position to propose a *terminus a quo* for the commision, but only after we have looked at 15:16–17 which tells us when Jeremiah accepted his call.

The separation of the call from the commission makes possible a younger age for Jeremiah at the time of call. The Heb *na'ar* means "boy," which is Bright's translation and now also the translation of the NRSV. So far as age goes the call of Jeremiah is best compared to the call of Samuel, for Samuel too was a "boy" when Yahweh first spoke to him (Heb *na'ar* in 1 Sam 2:11, 18, 21, 26; 3:1, 8). An age of 12 or 13 years would seem here to be about right.

At this particular point the parallel between Jeremiah and Moses has been overdrawn. Moses and Jeremiah both demur when Yahweh calls them, claiming speech limitations (Ex 4:10–17; cf. Jer 1:6), but Moses at the time is a grown man. Before the theophany at the burning bush he is big enough and strong enough to kill an Egyptian, separate two fighting Hebrews, and drive away pesty shepherds who are preventing women from drawing water in Midian (Ex 2:11–22). This takes place, according to Ex 2:11, "when Moses had grown up" (Heb *wayigdal mōšeh*). Jerome says the difference in age between Moses and Jeremiah explains the different responses of Yahweh to their respective demurs. Moses was rebuked because he was in his prime. Jeremiah, by contrast, was treated with leniency because at a young age fear and timidity are considered admirable traits.[5]

This rhetorical structure of chapter 1 gives the call a vision, which is not surprising with the hint already of a visionary experience in 1:9 where Yahweh stretches forth his hand to touch Jeremiah's mouth. Isaiah and Ezekiel had visions accompanying their calls (Isaiah 6; Ezekiel 1–3). Here, in the case of Jeremiah, the vision before a budding tree reinforces the connection with Moses, who, when he was called had a vision in front of a burning bush (Ex 3:1–6). Yahweh's concluding words, "I am watching over my word to do it" (1:12), create a sense of expectancy. Jeremiah is left thinking that the word he has just heard awaits a fulfillment. Things are not complete as they stand. Yahweh has something more in store for young Jeremiah.

We might conclude as much from Jeremiah's end of the dialogue, for nowhere is there any hint of the call being accepted, certainly nothing approaching Isaiah's "Here am I, send me" (Isa 6:8). We have long recognized that Jeremiah puts up resistance to the divine summons, but usually it is assumed that the hesitation was short-lived, and soon after Jeremiah was standing before Yahweh receiving his commission to begin ministry. But a better reading of the text is one which sees Jeremiah's acceptance of the call and Yahweh's commissioning for public ministry as still a ways off.

## JEREMIAH'S ACCEPTANCE OF THE CALL (15:16-17)

Jeremiah alludes to his acceptance of the call in one of his confessions, where, it seems, the need has arisen for the call to be renewed.[6] The confession is in 15:15–21 and reads in its entirety:

---

5. *S. Hieronymi Presbyteri Opera, In Hieremiam IV* (Turnhout: Brepols, 1960), 5: "Detestatur officium, quod pro aetate non potest sustinere, eadem uerecundia, qua et Moses tenuis et gracilis uocis esse se dicit. Sed ille quasi magnae robustaeque aetatis corripitur, huic pueritiae datur uenia, quae uerecundia et pudore decoratur."

6. Rowley, "The Early Prophecies of Jeremiah," 221–222.

## The Early Career of the Prophet Jeremiah

> ¹⁵O LORD, you know
>   remember me and visit me
>   and bring down retribution for me on my persecutors
> In your forbearance do not take me away
>   know that on your account I suffer insult
> ¹⁶Your words were found, and I ate them
>   and your words became to me a joy
> and the delight of my heart
>   for I am called by your name
>     O LORD, God of hosts
> ¹⁷I did not sit in the company of merrymakers
>   nor did I rejoice
> under the weight of your hand I sat alone
>   for you had filled me with indignation
> ¹⁸Why is my pain unceasing
>   my wound incurable
>   refusing to be healed?
> Truly, you are to me like a deceitful brook
>   like waters that fail.
>
> ¹⁹Therefore thus says the LORD:
> If you turn back, I will take you back
>   and you shall stand before me
> If you utter what is precious, and not what is worthless
>   you shall serve as my mouth
> It is they who will turn to you
>   not you who will turn to them
> ²⁰And I will make you to this people
>   a fortified wall of bronze
> they will fight against you
>   but they shall not prevail over you
> for I am with you
>   to save you and rescue you
>     says the LORD
> ²¹I will deliver you out of the hand of the wicked
>   and redeem you from the grasp of the ruthless.

This confession is an angry outburst in which Jeremiah complains that his call to be Yahweh's prophet has brought him much anguish. What troubles him more is that he accepted with joy.

## An Early Career Beginning at the Height of the Reform: A New View

Yahweh answers with a rebuke, telling Jeremiah in essence that he must "return" or "repent". If he does, Yahweh will reconfirm the promise made in both the call and the commission to spare Jeremiah the full measure of his enemies' wrath. He will be delivered. Bright says that vv 19-21 "clearly have the sound of a second call."[7]

Verse 16 speaks about "words" which Jeremiah ate, reminding one of the call of Ezekiel where that prophet ate words off a scroll given him by Yahweh (Ezek 2:8-3:3). The phrase, "for I am called by your name," in 16b suggests that Jeremiah has become Yahweh's possession, another reflection, perhaps, on the call.[8]

In verse 17 Jeremiah talks about isolating himself from some crowd of happy folk, which again could parallel Ezekiel's experience, but only to the extent that both individuals find it necessary to be alone after a divine visitation. Ezekiel, after he had eaten his scroll, sat overwhelmed among fellow exiles for seven days (Ezek 3:15). If he sat without speaking, which is commonly assumed (cf. Job 2:13), that would be an isolation of sorts. But the people with whom he sat were as downcast as he; Ezekiel was not with "merrymakers"—which actually would strengthen the parallel with Jeremiah, not weaken it. In any case, Jeremiah shunned the happy crowd because he was "under the weight of [Yahweh's] hand." Ezekiel too, after eating his scroll, felt the strong "hand" of Yahweh upon him (Ezek 3:14).

The clearest echoes of chapter 1 come, however, in vv 19-20. In v 19 Yahweh paraphrases 1:9, saying that Jeremiah will be his mouth, and v 20 is a but a reduced version of 1:18-19, the promise about rendering Jeremiah a "fortified wall of bronze" against all opposition. Verse 20 also repeats the assurance of deliverance in 1:8.

The important verse, so far as acceptance of the call is concerned, and the most difficult for interpretation, surely, is v 16, the first phrase of which reads in the MT:

---

7. Bright, *Jeremiah*, 112.

8. Erhard Gerstenberger, "Jeremiah's Complaints: Observations on Jer 15:10-21," *JBL* 82 (1963), 401.

The Early Career of the Prophet Jeremiah

*nimṣĕ'û dĕbāreykā wā'ōkĕlēm*

your words were found and I ate them

The Greek gives a paraphrastic reading which need not delay us. The MT is followed by the Targum, the other main versions of antiquity including the Vulgate, and virtually all modern translations. The NEB translated the LXX, but the REB returns to reading the MT. The MT is perfectly clear. The only difficulty really is the verb *mṣ'*, "found". What exactly is meant by "your words *were found*"? As was mentioned earlier, if Jeremiah is referring to the word of call we should expect rather *hyh*, "came", which is what appears in 1:4. McKane, who stays close to the MT, translates "your words came to me and I ate them."[9]

As was mentioned earlier I made the suggestion, now several years ago, that the phrase, "your words were found and I ate them," recalled the finding of the lawbook in the temple and Jeremiah's eating of those words, which Holladay accepted and used to support his low chronology.[10] But the low chronology has problems, as we have already pointed out. So also are there problems in Holladay's exegesis of 15:16–17. While it is conceivable to read the colon the way Holladay does, with the eating coming 13 (or 7) years after the finding, better sense is made if the eating comes right away. Ezekiel ate his scroll as soon as he received it from Yahweh. And also, what about the "joy and delight" said to have accompanied the eating? If Jeremiah's heart was joyful when he received the call, why is he portrayed in chapter 1 as being fearful and resistant? Holladay despite his reinterpretation of 1:2 still accepts 1:4–10 as the narrative of call. He says 1:9 is the "thought link" between the words found and the words eaten.[11] In any case, Jeremiah says that Yahweh's words were received with joy, and there is no hint of joy anywhere in 1:4–10. In fairness to Holladay, however, it should be pointed out that this is a

---

9. McKane, *Jeremiah I*, 350, 353.
10. See note 27 in chapter 2.
11. Jeremiah and Moses: Further Observations," 25.

## An Early Career Beginning at the Height of the Reform: A New View

problem facing anyone who finds in 15:16 a reflection on the call of chapter 1.

We actually do not need the low chronology in order to take 15:16 as a reference to the finding of the lawbook, at least not when the issuance of call is separated from the call's acceptance and the commission to begin ministry. Concluding as we did that the call was not accepted when issued by the young Jeremiah, we are now in a position to integrate 15:16–17 into our reconstruction. Acceptance of the call takes place in 622, when Jeremiah eats the words of the temple scroll. Now even more than before he understands himself to be the "prophet like Moses" of Deut 18:18. The eating takes place as soon as Jeremiah has had a chance to hear the scroll, and the "joy and delight" come when the words enter his mouth. Jeremiah may be reflecting Psa 119:103, which says:

> How sweet are your words to my taste
> sweeter than honey to my mouth!

Ezekiel found that the words he ate were "sweet as honey" in his mouth, but after they entered the stomach they became bitter (Ezek 3:3, 14; cf. Rev 10:8–11). The same thing happened to Jeremiah. Yahweh's words were sweet in his mouth (in 622), but after being assimilated they caused him great pain. Here, however, the bitterness comes later. Ezekiel's bitterness set in early.

We conclude then that Jeremiah's happy acceptance of Yahweh's call came not in 627 when Yahweh first spoke to him, but in an experience after the lawbook's finding in 622. The words of this scroll were for him the promised words of 1:9, mentioned also in the promise of Deut 18:18 which Yahweh had vouchsafed not simply for a future prophet but for an entire nation.

What were the words on the scroll which Jeremiah ate? Were they from Deuteronomy, i.e., words of Deuteronomic law? If so, then Jeremiah must be seen as a deep imbiber of Deuteronomic law, which taxes the imagination just a bit. The reconstruction proposed here does not depend on what was written on that scroll, still it would be nice to know. If the temple scroll did contain the Song of Moses in Deuteronomy 32, as I have suggested, then the words which Jeremiah consumes are precisely the ones which show up soon after in the preaching of chapter 2.

## THE COMMISSION TO BEGIN A PUBLIC MINISTRY (1:13-19)

If Jeremiah's acceptance of the call is dated to the finding of the lawbook in 622, we can now return to chapter 1 and complete the sequence of events leading up to the beginning of a public career. We left off in 1:12, where Yahweh said, "I am watching over my word to do it." What was this promised word, and when did Yahweh fulfill it?

One could say that the temple lawbook was a fulfillment of Yahweh's promise. The words of the lawbook were Yahweh's words, and Jeremiah by eating them could be said to have been eating words which were promised him in 1:9. Such an interpretation is possibly supported in the LXX of 1:12, which has "words" plural: "I am watching over my words to do them." But the MT reading "word" points in a different direction. It looks ahead to fulfillment in the next verse, 1:13, where it says, "and the word of the LORD came to me a second time." According to this reading the second vision is a fulfillment of the first and the commission is a fulfillment of the call.[12]

We said earlier that the commission narrative comprises all of 1:13-19, i.e., it includes the vision of the tilted pot about to spill over from the north. Verses 17-19 are the specific words of commission. This narrative of the commission contains verbal links to the narrative of call, further supporting the MT-supported link between vv 12 and 13. In 1:7 Yahweh had told Jeremiah, "all that I command you you shall speak (*wĕʾēt kol-ʾăšer ʾăṣawwĕkā tĕdabbēr*)." Now Yahweh says in 1:17: "and you shall

---

12. Lundbom, "Rhetorical Structures in Jeremiah 1," 209.

speak to them all that I command you" (*wĕdibbartâ ʾălêhem ʾēt kol-ʾăšer ʾānōkî ʾăṣawwekā*). Also in the call he said, "Do not be afraid of them" (1:8). Now in the commission he says, "Do not break down before them" (1:17).

Yahweh's commission speech promises that Jeremiah will be made into a "fortified city, an iron pillar, and bronze walls." This is necessary because the ministry to which he has been called will be a battle against kings, princes, priests, and the people of the land. A portent of this conflict is contained also in v 8 of the call: "Do not be afraid of them." And in v 10 Jeremiah is given the weighty responsibility of being set over "nations and over kingdoms, to pluck up and to pull down, to destroy and to overthrow, to build and to plant." Conflict here is a foregone conclusion. The final promise of salvation in v 19, "for I am with you, says the LORD, to deliver you," repeats the promise of 1:8. This continuity of language and ideas supports the view that the commission intends to be a reaffirmation of the call. Reaffirmation will come again in Jeremiah's mid-life crisis of 15:15–21.

When was the commission given? After Jeremiah's acceptance, most likely, which we have dated to 622 B.C. This date then becomes the *terminus a quo* for the giving of the commission and the beginning of a public career. In dating the beginning of the early career to 622 or shortly thereafter, we now have the prophet embarking on a public ministry not before, not after, but at the very climax of the Josianic Reform. If Jeremiah was 12 or 13 when the call came, he would begin his career at about 18, which is an acceptable age. These, of course, are only estimates. The ages could be higher, but they are not likely to be lower.

This new reconstruction brings substantive change to the traditional view. Jeremiah receives his call when he is a young boy, not a grown man. Acceptance takes place in 622, with the commission to begin ministry following soon after. Jeremiah does not then anticipate any phase of the reform, for no preaching is done between 627 and 622. Nor during these years does Jeremiah receive a vision of or announce the arrival of any early foe from the north. These adjustments take the major strain off the traditional view, and they do so without tampering with the chronological notices in 1:2; 25:1–3; and 36:1–2.

# 4

# A Trajectory of Jeremiah's Early Career

JEREMIAH WAS BORN ABOUT 640 B.C. in Anathoth, a village 2–3 miles north of Jerusalem where his father Hilkiah was priest at the village sanctuary. Hilkiah was likely a descendant of Abiathar, the priest of David whom Solomon retired to Anathoth after he became king (1 Kgs 2:26–27). The family possessed land (32:6–9). By tradition, and earlier by virtue of its location within the territory of Benjamin, Anathoth belonged to northern Israel, though now it was nothing more than a satellite community to Judah's capital city.

The year 640 saw Josiah accede to the Jerusalem throne at the age of 8 years. Those who placed him there did so with the aim of turning the nation in a new direction—away from Assyrian domination and back towards the ancient Yahwistic faith. That same year King Ashurbanipal of Assyria regained control over an empire which for 15 years had been in rebellion—since 655 when Psammetichus I of Egypt declared his independence. Nevertheless, Judah was now in possession of a political and religious freedom it had not enjoyed for many decades, and those guiding the young king were of a decidedly different spirit than Jerusalem's elite under the pro-Assyrian Manasseh, who died after a long reign in 642 B.C.

## The Early Career of the Prophet Jeremiah

Of Jeremiah's earliest years in Anathoth we know virtually nothing, save what Jeremiah tells us about his father being glad the day he was born (20:15). With Hilkiah being a priest we may assume for Jeremiah a religious upbringing, one in which he learned first-hand and from an early age the essentials of Yahweh worship and Israel's sacral traditions.

Jeremiah's boyhood had its similarities to that of Samuel, which was lived out at the Shiloh sanctuary not far from Anathoth. Traditions about Samuel and Israel's first sanctuary were doubtless preserved at Anathoth, where the priestly line of Abiathar could be traced back through to Eli, and beyond that to Moses. Jeremiah would have heard about Yahweh's call of Samuel, while he was yet a boy, which led finally to his becoming a prophet. Shiloh's destruction would also have been recounted to the young Jeremiah. Had he lived elsewhere the details of this unhappy event may not have been available, maybe the incident itself forgotten, unmentioned as it was in the sacral traditions—save Psa 78:60—where the memory was evidently too painful to preserve. Should this cryptic line in the psalm have raised questions in the mind of the young Jeremiah, an older priest—or Jeremiah's own father, for that matter—could certainly be counted on to have provided him with answers. Anathoth, being a northern sanctuary, would have been a storehouse of traditions about the northern prophets—Moses, Samuel, Elijah, Elisha, Hosea and others. Moses, Samuel, and Hosea made the strongest impression on Jeremiah's young mind, and as the years passed these came to influence him the most.

Either at Anathoth or at Jerusalem Jeremiah heard recited the stories of creation, the epics of the Fathers, and other portions of the sacred writings. Jerusalem was home to the nation's rich musical tradition, particularly as it expressed itself in the temple psalmbook. In the Jerusalem temple Jeremiah heard the antiphonal voices of the choirs, the priests reciting liturgies together with the congregation in sacred worship.

Out in the courtyard he may have heard, while still a boy, someone the people called a prophet, Zephaniah by name, a man of royal blood, who, in the spirit of Amos was fearlessly proclaiming an imminent day of Yahweh. Also like Amos, who spoke out boldly against Bethel and Samaria, and Isaiah too who was the presence to be reckoned with in Jerusalem less than a century ago, this Zephaniah made frontal attacks on idolatry and religious practices alien to the ancient Yahwistic faith, but which had thrived during the evil reign of Manasseh and were slow to die. Jeremiah may have been present, or else he heard about the day when Zephaniah called on people, in solemn assembly, to seek Yahweh and his righteousness (Zeph 2:1–4).

In 628, four years after Josiah "began to seek the God of David his father" (2 Chr 34:3a), the nation was sufficiently awakened for Josiah to carry out a purge of religious practices which had taken root during the years of Assyrian domination, practices associated not only with Assyrian worship but with the more localized worship of Baal (2 Chr 34:3b–7). The gods of Assyria were now repudiated, an action tantamount to a declaration of independence. Bold steps were possible only because Assyria had lost control of the western portion of her empire, and Judah was now largely in charge of her own destiny. Ashurbanipal died the next year, with Babylon to the south in open revolt. In October, 626, Nabopolassar of Babylon defeated the Assyrian army outside the city of Babylon.

Josiah took control over the northern provinces which Assyria had abandoned, also territories along the coastal plains. Worship centers there were destroyed or closed down. How Anathoth fared during the purge of 628 is not known. By 622 sanctuary life in both northern and southern towns were eliminated and worship centralized in Jerusalem (2 Kgs 23:8, 23). Anathoth by now would have been closed down.

The document inspiring the purge of 628 may have been an early edition of the book of Deuteronomy, perhaps chapters 1–28, although it is widely believed that proto-Deuteronomy was

## The Early Career of the Prophet Jeremiah

the "lost" scroll found in the temple in 622. But if the major purge was in 628 as the Chronicler indicates, not in 622, what other legislation besides Deuteronomy could have provided impetus and direction? This document, in any case, originated in the north and preached with the full authority of Moses the importance of covenant obedience.

After Samaria's fall, in 722, it was brought south where it played a major role in Hezekiah's reform during the closing years of the 8th c. (2 Kgs 18:1–6; 2 Chronicles 29–31). In this document Moses—who is the speaker almost entirely—makes his teaching contemporary. Priests in their public readings assumed the role of Moses. Jeremiah too identified with this towering figure out of Israel's past—a person of such stature that in the official view he was now *prophet par excellence* (see the post-622 appraisal of Deut 34:10–12). Jeremiah may well have heard an earlier Deuteronomy read at Anathoth, for it is unlikely that only one copy was vouchsafed to the temple in Jerusalem.

In the 13th year of Josiah, 627 B.C., when Jeremiah was perhaps 13 years old, Yahweh spoke to him at Anathoth, not in the sanctuary, but in the out-of-doors. Jeremiah had been chosen to be a prophet, not this day nor indeed years earlier when he lay hidden in his mother's womb. The choice was made before he was conceived, at a time known only to Yahweh. On this day, however, Yahweh was conveying the call and designating him for holy office. A similar thing happened to David when Yahweh called and designated him to be king. He was still young. On that solemn occasion the anointing was done by Samuel.

Jeremiah resisted the divine call now when it came to him, claiming he was too young and unable to speak. Yahweh overruled him, however, and after a word of assurance promptly designated him the "prophet like Moses" (Deut 18:18). Remembering the demur of Moses, made in part for the same reason, Yahweh answered him in appropriate fashion. No words of acceptance were offered, but Jeremiah's life from this day forth would be lived with a new sense of expectancy.

In the vision accompanying this experience Yahweh pointed Jeremiah to a budding almond tree. It was late January or early February. The branch was a sign that Yahweh would watch over his word to fulfill it. Yahweh realized, even more than Jeremiah, that things were not yet complete; some time needed to pass before words could be put into Jeremiah's mouth and prophetic work could begin. An affinity with Moses was now even more apparent when Jeremiah recalled that Moses received his call before a burning bush (Ex 3:1–14). Jeremiah could have understood this visitation in relation to a departing king, as Isaiah had done (Isa 6:1), for that year Ashurbanipal died. But Isaiah was not the prominent figure for Jeremiah. The prominent figure was Moses.

We do not know what Jeremiah was about between 627 and 622, except that he was not preaching. Yahweh's words had not yet been put into his mouth and he had not been sent out. During this time he was 13 to 18 years of age, according to the revised chronology. Jeremiah could have been in school, perhaps the scribal school in Jerusalem over which Shaphan presided. By the time he begins his ministry he is fully literate and well-trained in the rhetoric of his day. Later we find him also capable of writing scrolls as scribes were trained to do (30:2; 36:2; 51:60). The lifelong bond between Jeremiah and members of the Shaphan family, which endured through particularly hard times (Ahikam in 26:24; Elasah in 29:3; Gemariah in 36:11–12, 25; and Gedaliah in 39:14; 40:5–6), may well have had its origin here. At some point early in life Jeremiah made the move to Jerusalem. When his ministry begins the locus of his activity is here. Actually, there is not much of an audience at Anathoth; the place is small and by 622 the sanctuary is closed down. Jeremiah's audience is at the Jerusalem temple.

The year 622 B.C. was one of great excitement in Jerusalem. While renovations were being made in the temple, Hilkiah, the high priest, found a "book of the law." He showed it to Shaphan who read it first to himself and then to the king. The king, upon hearing its words, was deeply moved, enough so to rend his clothes. These were Yahweh's words, and had behind them also the authority of Moses, the great lawgiver in Israel (2 Chr 34:14; cf. 2 Kgs 23:25).

The temple scroll is not a call for covenant obedience, nor even a warning about non-compliance, which is what Deuteronomy 1–28 contains. It is instead a judgment upon a nation guilty of covenant disobedience. Josiah was quick to perceive the implications, both for himself and for the nation. An interpretation for the contemporary situation was urgent, and the scroll was therefore taken to a prophetess named Huldah who lived in Jerusalem. She obliged with a two-pronged oracle, the first part directed to the nation and the second part to the king (2 Kgs 22:16–20). The portion to the nation updated a judgment in Deut 32:15–22, where it said that Israel was under indictment because she has forgotten Yahweh and made him angry by sacrificing to other gods. Because of this the divine wrath would burn like an unquenchable fire. Judgment upon the nation was clear. Josiah in his portion of the oracle received mercy, because he humbled himself. Mercy extended even to his death. Huldah said he would not see the evil slated for Jerusalem. The times did not look good. The prophet Zephaniah had said as much.

Huldah's oracle, as well as what was written on the temple scroll, were soon public knowledge in Jerusalem. Jeremiah heard them along with everyone else. The words of the scroll had their own particular impact on Jeremiah. For him they were the words Yahweh promised to put into his mouth (1:9). He therefore consumed them with great delight, despite the fact that what he was eating were words of harsh judgment. The bitterness would come later (15:18). Judgment, of course, was new neither to him nor to the people. Jerusalem had heard it from a line of prophets some of whom called the city home. There were Nathan, Isaiah, Micah of Moresheth, and now just recently Zephaniah whose dire predictions everyone had heard.

Jeremiah, for his part, had been warned of judgment when the call came and he was given by Yahweh the power of agency to bring it to pass (1:10). However frightful the prediction seemed—and we must believe it was frightful—people could repent and Yahweh would show mercy. Jeremiah, in any event, is now joyful for a time. He is happy to be called by Yahweh's name (15:16), and it gives him pleasure to know that Yahweh has followed through on his promise to put words into his mouth. Jeremiah was in readiness. When the words turned up on the temple scroll it seemed right for him to eat them. Now the call to be Yahweh's prophet was accepted.

If Jeremiah's feeling of joy was mingled with apprehension and unease about the future, the same must be said for the king and others in Judah, only more so. Much celebrating took place in Jerusalem. There was a ceremony of covenant renewal and a grand celebration of passover, the likes of which had not been seen for many a year (2 Kgs 23:21–23; 2 Chr 35:1–19). But the level of anxiety also ran high. Josiah's reason for leading the nation in covenant renewal was to ward off disaster. Everyone knew that. The purge of alien religious practices—now or earlier—was perhaps done for the same reason, though we cannot be sure what provided the impetus in 628.

The Song of Moses, which caused the initial consternation in the halls of government, was deemed important enough to become the nucleus for an expansion to the book of Deuteronomy, i.e., chapters 29–34. It was, after all, a lawsuit of sorts which sued Israel for breach of covenant. In the expansion the Song was given a context: Moses' farewell address in the plains of Moab. It was also given the designation of "torah" or "law" (Deut 31:24, 26; 32:46), enabling it to be ranked with the rest of Deuteronomy which was already established "torah" from Moses (Deut 1:5; 4:44).

Jeremiah distanced himself from the merriment going on in the city, perhaps not taking part in the covenant renewal or passover festivities. The popular response may have been judged by him to be superficial in light of Yahweh's ominous words. Later he recalls being filled with indignation at the time (15:17). Others boycotted the Jerusalem celebration though probably for a different reason (2 Kgs 23:9), that being an objection to worship now at a single sanctuary. Jeremiah was akin in spirit to Huldah. For whatever reason, Jeremiah sat alone.

If Jeremiah's relationship with Jerusalem's ruling elite was ambiguous, the same cannot be said for his relationship with Yahweh, at least not now. Yahweh spoke to him again, this time telling him a foe was poised to attack Judah from the north. The word was conveyed in a vision which came as Jeremiah stood before a tipped pot, its contents about ready to spill out. The pot faced away from the north. With this announcement came also a personal message: Jeremiah must now begin his work as a prophet (1:13–19). Jeremiah remembered that Yahweh said he would watch over his word to do it. Now he has done it. The promise concluding the call is fulfilled.

Jeremiah learns that the foe will come to the very gates of Jerusalem, worse yet it will take up residence there. The people must be told this, which is what brought Yahweh to commission Jeremiah. But Jeremiah will have a battle of his own to contend with, for spirited opposition can be expected from just about everyone. But that must not dismay him. Yahweh promises him what he will not promise Jerusalem: protection. Those who fight against him will not prevail; Yahweh will be with Jeremiah and see that his life is spared. This vision came to Jeremiah in 622 or shortly after, once the lawbook had been found and once the call was accepted.

On the strength of Yahweh's promise Jeremiah begins his career as a prophet. He now goes to the courtyard of the temple where prophets customarily go to give their oracles. He stands somewhere to the side, in view and within hearing distance of people who are on their way in or out of the temple. There he speaks the words Yahweh has put into his mouth. Some come into the courtyard just to see what is going on, and they hear him. Jeremiah's oracles are short; most can be spoken in 30 seconds or less. He may link two, three, or four oracles together, as poets do today when reading their poems in public. The oracles and utterances of other description are short because people have only a moment or two to stop and listen. Then they move on. There is nothing in this preaching approaching a modern-day sermon. In fact, the term "sermon" is inappropriate—even for the so-called "Temple Sermon" of 7:1–15, which, upon closer inspection, is seen to break down into three temple oracles: vv 3–7, 8–11, and 12–15. Because the audience is constantly changing Jeremiah repeats his oracles. After many deliveries they become like "polished stones." At the same time they can change slightly from one day's delivery to the next.

In his earliest preaching, a portion of which is preserved in 2:1–4:4, Jeremiah picks up on the reform themes of idolatry and religious harlotry. His rootage in traditions from the north is apparent, even to the point of coloring traditions which he appropriates from the south, e.g., in 4:1–2 when he says that the blessings of the Abraham covenant are contingent upon Israel's repentance. The contingent nature of the covenant he no doubt learned from Deuteronomy, but that was the Sinai covenant made with Israel and mediated through Moses. The Abraham covenant contained no such conditions.

One meets up with youthful idealism in the early preaching, although this may be simply the romanticism of the age which was widespread and affected more or less everyone. We see this in the oracle in 2:2–3, which paints Israel's wilderness experience as idyllic. It continues in 2:5–9, where Jeremiah borrows diction from the Song of Moses in attacking the sorry condition of covenant life. There is conceptual borrowing as well, e.g., when he contrasts Yahweh's goodness in the exodus, wanderings, and settlement to Israel's blatant ingratitude, or when he pinpoints Israel's settlement in the land as the time when things began to go bad (cf. Deut 32:10–18).

Jeremiah shows a clear understanding of the conditional nature of the Sinai covenant as set forth in Deuteronomy 1–28, but he goes beyond it, saying that disobedience *has* taken place and the curses *will* come to pass. In expressing the covenant as a familial bond—between husband and wife or between father and son—he betrays indebtedness to Hosea. There is influence also from Hosea at the point where Jeremiah casts the nation as an adulterous wife.

This early preaching is done in the spirit of the reform, and to that extent it supports a program now well along. Reforms initiated at the highest levels of state still have to be brought to the people. At the same time Jeremiah's preaching is targeted not so much at effecting external change—which was the practical outcome if not the stated goal of Josiah's program—but at bringing about a change in the human heart. Without Jeremiah's call for repentance and a circumcision of the heart there could be no covenant renewal. Without the same would also come national ruin. Jeremiah is privy to Yahweh's plan regarding a foe from the north, and his reform preaching is done with the knowledge that should repentance not come about, destruction will. In this respect his preaching is little different from that of the legendary Jonah, who of course witnessed results dramatically different (Jonah 3). Jeremiah's eloquent plea for repentance and reform in 4:1–4 is fully in the spirit of the reform of 622, and after.

That Jeremiah supported certain reform goals and objectives can be inferred from his preaching on covenant obedience (11:1–8), and the call which he made for more rigorous sabbath observance (17:19–27). The latter in no way compromises the higher ethical and moral principles which he championed. Both of these speeches fit well in the period after 622. Jeremiah reflects current nationalistic sentiment to the extent that he wants Judah divested of its vassalage to Assyria and Egypt (2:18, 36; 13:1–11), and the exiles taken away to Assyria in 722 returned home (3:12–13; 31:2–20). Jeremiah supports political reunion of north and south, and in connection with which he is likely to have gone along with Josiah's plan for a single sanctuary in Jerusalem (3:14; 31:2–14). If he supported the latter a reason exists for the hostility of kin early in his career. These kin—who were priests—had become marginalized if not put out of work entirely by the closing of the Anathoth sanctuary (11:18–12:6).

Though Jeremiah is depicted at various points as being a solitary individual, even saying of himself that he shunned crowds and "sat alone," it would be a mistake to draw the broader conclusion that his ministry was carried on detached from things going on around him, or that he remained aloof and independent of others, who, at the same time were giving attention to precisely the concerns he was. It is best to think of Jeremiah's isolation at the time of the 622 celebration as being short-lived. During the Josianic years he was otherwise active in pursuing his vocation as a prophet—preaching, attending temple worship, and associating with a wide range of people in the capital city.

Even though early in his career Jeremiah acted on a mandate given him by Yahweh, his actions were carried out in concert with all sorts of people—prophets some of them—who shared the hope that Judah would take advantage of the opportunity it now had to renew commitment to the ancient Yahwistic faith. His call in 4:1–4 for a return to Yahweh and a circumcision of the heart had found expression already in Deut 4:30 and 10:16.

Like his predecessor, Zephaniah, and other prophets soon to be his contemporaries, if they were not contemporaries already, Habakkuk and Nahum, Jeremiah was an active participant in temple worship and led people, at various times, in temple liturgies. We must, of course, imagine tension every now and then between him and those of the Jerusalem establishment, particularly priests and prophets, who, because they share Jeremiah's same station in society are naturally the most sensitive to what he is doing. On one occasion Jeremiah becomes angered because of what certain scribes are doing to the written torah (8:8). Jeremiah experienced tension with members of his own family—who again were priests—though we do not know precisely when. There was tension also with people in the society at large, and small wonder, when one considers that neither high nor low, professional nor non-professional, escaped his indictments (2:8; 5:4–5).

## The Early Career of the Prophet Jeremiah

Sometime early in his career Jeremiah was told by Yahweh not to marry. He was also told not to attend weddings or wakes (16:1–9). The reason: war and mass destruction lay ahead. These were actions not likely to curry favor with those whose job it was to maintain community life and the present social order.

A second focus in Jeremiah's preaching during the early career—which may represent a second phase of ministry, though we cannot be sure—centered on the foe from the north. Jeremiah was apprised of this threat when his career began, but now he must prepare people to meet the unblessed event. Coming now from the prophet are oracles and poems announcing the foe, also laments over all the destruction which will result. The hurt will be deep, and everyone including Jeremiah must bear it. The legacy of these utterances is found in 4:5–6:30; 8:4–9:22[21]; and 10:17–22.

Laments in chapters 8–10 show Jeremiah involved at the deepest level of his preaching. Dialogues and trialogues rapidly alternate between divine word, cries of human terror, and the prophet's own outpouring of grief (8:13–17, 18–21). Some laments show profound loneliness (8:22–9:2[1]; 9:10–11[9–10]). Woven in are the earlier themes of idolatry, religious harlotry, and injustice—also inhumane behavior—which give Yahweh reason enough to bring judgment. Jeremiah at this point gives some unexpected twists to sacred traditions emanating from the south, e.g., his reversal of Yahweh's mighty work of creation (4:23–26; cf. Genesis 1), and his recast of Abraham's negotiation for the deliverance of Sodom, making it a negotiation for the pardon of Jerusalem (5:1–8; cf. Gen 18:22–33).

Utterances in the "foe cycle" probably came later than those addressing the reform, although we cannot be sure. The materials correlate best with Babylon's rise to power in Mesopotamia and Syria, which is ca. 614–609 B.C. Habakkuk announces the rise of this same foe in 615 or later. And we are not sure when Zephaniah issues his warning. But the foe poems taken as a whole span a period greater than 614–609; some could well have been spoken earlier, and some are definitely later because the enemy is threatening Judah at close range.

Jeremiah in preaching destruction creates tension between himself and others of his same office. The problem seems to be that prophets are proclaiming peace and national well-being (4:9–10; 5:12–13, 30–31; 6:13–15[=8:10b-12]). In 612, of course, there is much elation over the fall of Nineveh. Summing up the sentiment here is the prophet Nahum, who delivers his oracle about this time. Jeremiah is silent about Nineveh's fall. This cannot be due to an inability to express vengeance, for oracles coming later include vengeance upon most every nation of the world. Jeremiah's nationalistic sentiments are now likely muted because of having to preach judgment upon Judah.

In Josiah's later years Jeremiah becomes frustrated over the ineffectiveness of the reform. Josiah is now busy fortifying cities north and west of Jerusalem, e.g., Megiddo and Lachish. Jeremiah is also frustrated over his own ineffectiveness as a preacher. People have not heeded his call to return to the "ancient paths," i.e., the Mosaic covenant, nor have they listened to warnings he has given them about war and national destruction. The oracle of disillusionment in 6:16–21 gives a certain focus to the early career. In it Jeremiah expresses dissatisfaction over temple worship as well, which will give way to a frontal attack once Jehoiakim becomes king. There are other signs of disillusionment. Jeremiah says no real repentance has taken place (5:20–31; 8:4–7). In fact, the whole reform appears to have been insincere (3:6–11). Jeremiah himself has even become wayward during this troubled time, and has to be called back (15:19–21). The deep soul-searching going on in the confessions is Jeremiah's way of dealing with a ministry gone awry, or, if not gone awry then one which seems not to be going anywhere.

The Jeremianic confessions, which are laments really, begin in Josiah's reign but increase in number during the reign of Jehoiakim. Some are undoubtedly from the years 609–604 when Jeremiah was *persona non grata* with the new king. These confessions, which form the poetic substratum of chapters 11–20, may in many instances be contemporary with the general laments of chapters 8–10. Jeremiah uttered a lament for Josiah which did not survive (2 Chr 35:25), and another three months later for Jehoahaz which did (22:10–12). He appears to have been very moved when this young king was taken to Egypt, where he would die (cf. 2 Kgs 23:31–34).

These glimpses into the prophet's interior life show that bedrock tenets of faith were being called into question. Why should acceptance of the divine call lead to an intolerable wilderness experience where God was not present? (15:15–18). Had not Jeremiah spoken earlier about Israel's wilderness experience as a time of honeymoon with Yahweh? And was not Yahweh the fountain of living water, as Jeremiah also stated earlier? Preaching the divine word brings Jeremiah much anguish. It causes close friends to turn on him, which then leads him to claim betrayal by Yahweh (20:7–10). In the darkest hour of all Jeremiah rejects his birth, his call, and early assurrances that Yahweh would deliver him from all his enemies (20:14–18). Yet we find that once the hurts are let out, assurances are renewed (15:19–21) and Jeremiah too is renewed, even to the point where he is able to sing about Yahweh's deliverance (20:11–13).

Jeremiah was deeply involved in the religious life of his nation. What personal piety—also impiety—he manifests in the confessions is balanced off by active participation in cultic life. There is no privatizing of religion, as is sometimes alleged, for while Jeremiah prays for himself he prays even more for others. In fact, Yahweh has to tell him at one point to stop interceding (11:14–17; 14:11–12; 15:1–4). Jeremiah led temple liturgies of petition and confession, a sample of which are preserved in 3:21–25; 10:23–24; and 14:1–9, 19–22.

The death of Josiah was a national tragedy, and one of the great puzzlements is Jeremiah's silence about the Megiddo adventure. Perhaps he supported the king's action, which would have later caused him embarrassment. Jeremiah's earlier demeaning of Assyria and Egypt, and his openly pro-Babylonian sympathies later, could point to such a conclusion. It is astonishing, really, to hear the Chronicler report that the only words to come from the mouth of God were those spoken by Neco, who told Josiah not to oppose him (2 Chr 35:20–22). Was there no prophet in Jerusalem who could speak Yahweh's word? And why no word from Jeremiah? Only a lament, and a later remembrance of this good king when a comparison was made to his son Jehoiakim (22:13–17). Somehow what is *not said* in this situation speaks louder than what is.

The years from 609 to 604 were difficult for the prophet, as the dated prose now beginning to appear in the book makes clear. When Neco installed Jehoiakim the political climate in Jerusalem changed, for Judah was now under Egyptian domination. National independence was at an end and Judah was put under heavy taxation. The reform was also over, as we can surmise from the celebrated temple oracles which Jeremiah delivered in Jehoiakim's accession year (26:1).

On this occasion Jeremiah made a scathing indictment of the people's shallow religiosity and duplicity before Yahweh (7:1–15). People, it seems, were content simply to know that the temple stood tall on Mt. Zion and that salvific liturgies were being said in worship. They cared nothing about executing justice or living in accordance with covenant demands. Jeremiah says Jerusalem was rife with every imaginable evil. But the real nerve was struck when Jeremiah announced that Yahweh was about to destroy the temple as he destroyed Shiloh. This silenced the prophet and court was quickly called into session at the New Gate. Jeremiah was put on trial.

The priests and the prophets, who were the most offended and who were also, no doubt, providing cover for the king as Amaziah did earlier for Jeroboam II (Amos 7:10–13), made up the prosecution. They demanded that Jeremiah be put to death. Princes in attendance seemed allied with the defense. In the end the princes decided the case since the king was not present. The verdict was rendered in Jeremiah's favor. They accepted Jeremiah's testimony that Yahweh had sent him with the message just delivered. For them Jeremiah passed the test of a true prophet set forth in Deut 13:1–5. Some elders present also aided the defense by recalling that Micah earlier predicted the destruction of Jerusalem, and King Hezekiah did not put him to death.

So Jeremiah survived the trial. Still he needed the special protection of Ahikam, son of Shaphan (26:24), probably in order to be spared the wrath of those who brought him to trial, not to mention the wrath of the king. Another Yahweh prophet, Uriah of Kiriath-jearim, delivered a similar judgment on the city and Jehoiakim had him killed (26:20–23).

According to our reckoning Jeremiah is about 31 years old in 609 B.C. By now he is a familiar figure at the temple and well-known throughout Jerusalem. Sometime between 609 and 605 Jeremiah invited senior priests and other leading citizens to accompany him to the Valley of Ben-hinnom. There he gave an object lesson on apostasy and what its consequences would be (chapter 19). This incurred for him the wrath of Pashhur, a high-ranking temple priest, who took him into custody, beat him, and put him into stocks overnight (20:1–6). What we are seeing here is one priest's latent response to Jeremiah's temple oracles and a trial which did not go his way.

Jeremiah is again in the temple with a group of Rechabites early in the reign of Jehoiakim. The purpose is to give another object lesson, this one on fidelity and obedience to the covenant (chapter 35). In 605 Jeremiah is debarred from the temple, and he no doubt continued to absent himself from its precincts so long as Jehoiakim was king. During this same general period Jeremiah likely issued his personal attack on Jehoiakim for a reckless building program and unjust practices (22:13–17). Other remarks of a critical nature were made about the prophets (23:9–40). The confessions which conclude the First Edition of the book of Jeremiah (20:7–18) fit well about 605–604, a time when Jeremiah was facing opposition on a number of fronts.

The year 605 was pivotal, both for the nation and for Jeremiah personally. The Battle of Carchemish left Egypt weakened and Babylon the new power broker in world affairs. Jeremiah addressed the Egyptian defeat with an oracle (46:3–12). Another given this year or the next was spoken by Habakkuk (Hab 1:5–11). Now Babylon is identified as the foe from the north, and Jeremiah has the added temerity to call Nebuchadrezzar Yahweh's "servant" (25:9).

A decision is made in 605 to commit a collection of Jeremiah's utterances to writing. Jeremiah summons for the task a scribe named Baruch who writes up a scroll at his dictation (36:1–8). This scroll is a reduced version of chapters 1–20, i.e., the First Edition. A personal word of consolation and hope is given to Baruch (chapter 45). At one time this served as a colophon to the First Edition. In the next year, 604, Baruch reads the scroll in the temple on a fast day. The Babylonian army is now in the Philistine Plain busy destroying Ashkelon. Jeremiah composed an oracle in response to this event (47:2–7). When Jehoiakim heard the scroll, he defiantly cut it into strips and cast it into the fire. Baruch and Jeremiah had already been sent into hiding for now they were in direct conflict with the king (36:9–32). The early career had thus ended.

# Bibliography

Albright, William F. "The Biblical Period" in *The Jews: Their History, Culture and Religion I.* (ed. Louis Finkelstein; New York: Harper & Bros., 1955).

———. "Some Remarks on the Song of Moses in Deuteronomy XXXII," *VT* 9 (1959), 339-346 [= Noth 1959: 3-10].

Bardtke, Hans. "Jeremia der Fremdvölkerprophet," *ZAW* 53 (1935), 209-239; 54 (1936), 240-262.

Baumgartner, Walter. *Jeremiah's Poems of Lament.* (tr. David E. Orton; Sheffield: Sheffield Press, 1987). Originally 1917.

Berridge, John M. *Prophet, People, and the Word of Yahweh.* (Zürich: EVZ-Verlag, 1970).

Best, Thomas F. (ed.). *Hearing and Speaking the Word: Selections from the Works of James Muilenburg.* (Chico, CA: Scholars Press, 1984).

Bewer, Julius A. *The Book of Jeremiah I.* (New York: Harper & Bros., 1951).

Birkeland, Harris. "Grunddrag i profeten Jeremias förkunnelse," *SEÅ* 1 (1936), 31-46.

———. *Zum Hebräischen Traditionswesen: Die Komposition der prophetischen Bucher des Alten Testaments.* (Oslo: Jacob Dybwad, 1938).

Boadt, Lawrence. *Jeremiah 1-25.* (OTM 9; Wilmington, DE: Michael Glazier, 1982).

———. *Jeremiah 26-52, Habakkuk, Zephaniah, Nahum.* (OTM 10; Wilmington, DE: Michael Glazier, 1982).

Bogaert, Pierre-Maurice (ed.). *Le Livre de Jérémie, Le Prophète et son milieu les oracles et leur transmission.* (BETL 54; Leuven: Leuven University Press, 1981).

Bright, John. "The Date of the Prose Sermons of Jeremiah," *JBL* 70 (1951), 15-29 [= Perdue and Kovacs 1984: 193-212].

———. *Jeremiah.* (AB 21; Garden City, NY: Doubleday & Co., 1965).

———. *A History of Israel.* 3rd ed. (Philadelphia: Westminster Press, 1981).

Brueggemann, Walter. *To Pluck Up, To Tear Down: A Commentary on the Book of Jeremiah 1-25.* (ITC; Grand Rapids: Wm. B. Eerdmans Publishing Co., 1988).

———. *To Build, To Plant: A Commentary on Jeremiah 26-52.* (ITC; Grand Rapids: Wm. B. Eerdmans Publishing Co., 1991).

Budde, Karl. "Über das erste Kapitel des Buches Jeremia," *JBL* 40 (1921), 23-37.

## Bibliography

Calvin, John. *Commentaries on the Book of the Prophet Jeremiah and the Lamentations I-II.* (Grand Rapids: Baker Book House, 1979).
Carroll, Robert P. *From Chaos to Covenant.* (New York: Crossroad, 1981).
———. *The Book of Jeremiah.* (OTL; Philadelphia: Westminster Press, 1986).
Cazelles, Henri. "Zephaniah, Jeremiah, and the Scythians in Palestine" in Perdue and Kovacs 1984: 129-149 [= "Sophonie, Jérémie, et les Scythes en Palestine," *RB* 74 (1967), 24-44].
Cheyne, T. K. *Jeremiah: His Life and Times.* (London: James Nisbet & Co., 1888).
———. "Jeremiah" in *EncB* (11th ed.) 15, 323-325.
Childs, Brevard S. "The Enemy from the North and the Chaos Tradition," *JBL* 78 (1959), 187-198 [= Perdue and Kovacs 1984: 151-161].
Clements, R. E. *Jeremiah.* (Interpretation; Atlanta: John Knox Press, 1988).
Condamin, P. Albert. *Le Livre de Jérémie.* 3rd ed. (Paris: Librairie Lecoffre, 1936).
Cornill, D. Carl Heinrich. *Das Buch Jeremia.* (Leipzig: Chr. Herm. Tauchnitz, 1905).
Couturier, G. P. "Jeremiah" in *JBC*, 300-336.
Craigie, Peter C., Kelley, Page H., and Drinkard, Joel F. Jr. *Jeremiah 1-25.* (WBC 26; Dallas: Word Books, 1991).
Cross, Frank M. Jr., and Freedman, David Noel. "Josiah's Revolt against Assyria," *JNES* 12 (1953) 56-58.
Cunliffe-Jones, H. *The Book of Jeremiah.* (TBC; London: SCM Press, 1960).
Driver, S. R. *The Book of the Prophet Jeremiah.* (London: Hodder & Stoughton, 1906).
Duhm, D. Bernhard. *Das Buch Jeremia.* (KHC; Tübingen and Leipzig: Verlag von J. C. B. Mohr [Paul Siebeck], 1901).
Engnell, Ivan. "Jeremias bok" in *SBU* 1 (2nd ed.), 1098-1106.
Freedman, David Noel. "The Babylonian Chronicle," *BA* 19 (1956), 50-60 [= Wright and Freedman 1961: 113-127].
———. "Divine Commitment and Human Obligation," *Int* 18 (1964), 419-431 [= *Divine Commitment and Human Obligation* I; ed. John R. Huddlestun; Grand Rapids: Eerdmans, 1997, 168-178].
Freedman, Harry. *Jeremiah.* (London: Soncino Press, 1949).
Gadd, C. J. *The Fall of Nineveh.* (London: British Museum, 1923).
Gerstenberger, Erhard. "Jeremiah's Complaints: Observations on Jer 15:10-21," *JBL* 82 (1963), 393-408.
Giesebrecht, D. Fredrich. *Das Buch Jeremia.* 2nd ed. (HKAT; Göttingen: Vandenhoeck & Ruprecht, 1907). Originally 1894.
Gordon, T. C. "A New Date for Jeremiah," *ET* 44 (1932-33), 562-565.
Gottwald, Norman. *A Light to the Nations.* (New York: Harper & Bros., 1959).
Graf, Karl Heinrich. *Der Prophet Jeremia.* (Leipzig: T. O. Weigel, 1862).
Grant, Michael. *The History of Ancient Israel.* (New York: Charles Scribner's Sons, 1984).
Gross, Karl. *Die literarische Verwandtschaft Jeremias mit Hosea.* (Inaug. diss.; Borna-Leipzig: Universitätsverlag von Robert Noske, 1930).

# Bibliography

———. "Hoseas Einfluss auf Jeremias Anschauungen," *NKZ* 42 (1931), 241–256, 327–343.

Gunkel, Hermann. "Schriftstellerei und Formensprache der Propheten," in Gunkel, *Die Propheten*. (Göttingen: Vandenhoeck & Ruprecht, 1917), 104–140.

———. "The Secret Experiences of the Prophets," *The Expositor* 9th Series 1 (1924), 356–366; 427–435; 2 (1924), 23–32 [= "Die geheimen Erfahrungen der Propheten" in *Die Schriften des Alten Testaments II: Die großen Propheten* (ed. D. Hans Schmidt; Göttingen: Vandenhoeck und Ruprecht, 1923), xvii-xxxiv].

Hallo, William. "From Qarqar to Carchemish: Assyria and Israel in the Light of New Discoveries" in *The Biblical Archaeologist Reader II*. (eds. David Noel Freedman and Edward F. Campbell; Garden City, NY: Doubleday & Co., 1964), 152–188 [= *BA* 23 (1960), 34–61].

Hamilton, R. W. "Beth-shan" in *IDB* A-D, 397–401.

Henderson, E. *The Book of the Prophet Jeremiah and That of the Lamentations*. (London: Hamilton, Adams & Co., 1851).

Herrmann, Siegfried. *Jeremia*. (BK 12:1-2; Neukirchen-Vluyn: Neukirchener Verlag, 1986–1990).

———. *Jeremia: Der Prophet und das Buch*. (Darmstadt: Wissenschaftliche Buchgesellschaft, 1990).

Hitzig, F. *Der Prophet Jeremia*. 2nd ed. (Leipzig: Verlag von S. Hirzel, 1866). Originally 1841.

Holladay, William L. "The Background of Jeremiah's Self-Understanding: Moses, Samuel, and Psalm 22," *JBL* 83 (1964), 153–164 [= Perdue and Kovacs 1984: 313–324].

———. "Jeremiah and Moses: Further Observations," *JBL* 85 (1966), 17–27.

———. *Jeremiah: Spokesman Out of Time*. (Philadelphia: Pilgrim Press, 1974).

———. *The Architecture of Jeremiah 1-20*. (Lewisburg: Bucknell University Press, 1976).

———. "The Identification of the Two Scrolls of Jeremiah," *VT* 30 (1980), 452–467.

———. "A Coherent Chronology of Jeremiah's Early Career" in *Le Livre de Jérémie*. (ed. P.-M. Bogaert; Leuven: Leuven University Press, 1981), 58–73.

———. "The Years of Jeremiah's Preaching," *Int* 37 (1983), 146–159 [= Mays and Achtemeier 1987: 130–142].

———. *Jeremiah I*. (Hermeneia; Philadelphia: Fortress Press, 1986).

———. *Jeremiah II*. (Hermeneia; Minneapolis: Augsburg Fortress, 1989).

Horst, F. "Die Anfänge des Propheten Jeremia," *ZAW* 41 (1923), 94–153.

Hyatt, J. Philip. "The Peril from the North in Jeremiah," *JBL* 59 (1940), 499–513.

———. "Torah in the Book of Jeremiah," *JBL* 60 (1941), 381–396.

———. "Jeremiah and Deuteronomy," *JNES* 1 (1942), 156–173 [= Perdue and Kovacs 1984: 113–127].

———. "Jeremiah and War," *Crozer Quarterly* 20 (1943), 52–58.

*Bibliography*

———. "The Deuteronomic Edition of Jeremiah," *Vanderbilt Studies in the Humanities* 1 (1951), 71–95 [= Perdue and Kovacs 1984: 247–267].
———. "Jeremiah" in *IB* 5, 777–1142.
———. "The Beginning of Jeremiah's Prophecy," *ZAW* 78 (1966), 204–214 [= Perdue and Kovacs 1984: 63–72].
Japhet, Sara. "The Historical Reliability of Chronicles," *JSOT* 33 (1985), 83–107.
Jastrow, Morris Jr. "Babylonia and Assyria" in *EncB* (11th ed.) 3, 99–112.
[Jerome]. *S. Hieronymi Presbyteri Opera, In Hieremiam IV*. (Turnhout: Brepols, 1960).
Johnstone, W. "The Setting of Jeremiah's Prophetic Activity," *TGUOS* 21 (1965–66), 47–55.
Kessler, Martin. "A Prophetic Biography: A Form-Critical Study of Jer. 26–29, 32–45." (Unpublished Ph.D dissertation, Brandeis University, 1965).
———. "Form-Critical Suggestions on Jer 36," *CBQ* 28 (1966), 389–401.
Koch, Klaus. *The Growth of the Biblical Tradition*. (tr. S. M. Cupitt; New York: Charles Scribner's Sons, 1969).
Lemke, Werner E. "The Synoptic Problem in the Chronicler's History," *HTR* 58 (1965), 349–363.
Lipinski, Edward. "Jeremiah" in *EncJud* 9, 1345–1359.
Lohfink, Norbert. "Die Gattung der 'Historischen Kurzgeschichte' in den letzten Jahren von Juda und in der Zeit des Babylonischen Exils," *ZAW* 90 (1978), 319–347.
———. "Der junge Jeremia als Propagandist und Poet: Zum Grundstock von Jer 30–31" in *Le Livre de Jérémie*. (ed. Pierre-Maurice Bogaert; Leuven: Leuven University Press, 1981), 351–368.
Ludwig, Theodore M. "The Shape of Hope: Jeremiah's Book of Consolation," *CTM* 39 (1968), 526–541.
Lundbom, Jack R. *Jeremiah: A Study in Ancient Hebrew Rhetoric*. (SBLDS 18; Missoula, MT: Society of Biblical Literature and Scholars Press, 1975; 2nd ed. Winona Lake, IN: Eisenbrauns, 1997).
———. "The Lawbook of the Josianic Reform," *CBQ* 38 (1976), 293–302.
———. "The Double Curse in Jeremiah 20:14–18," *JBL* 104 (1985), 589–600.
———. "Baruch, Seraiah, and Expanded Colophons in the Book of Jeremiah," *JSOT* 36 (1986), 89–114.
———. "Scribal Colophons and Scribal Rhetoric in Deuteronomy 31–34" in *Haim M. I. Gevaryahu Memorial Volume*. (eds. Joshua J. Adler and B. Z. Luria; Jerusalem: World Jewish Bible Center, 1990), 53–63.
———. "Rhetorical Structures in Jeremiah 1," *ZAW* 103 (1991), 193–210.
———. "Jeremiah and the Break-Away from Authority Preaching," *SEÅ* 56 (1991), 7–28.
———. "Jeremiah (Prophet)" in *ABD* 3, 684–698.
———. "Jeremiah, Book of" in *ABD* 3, 706–721.
May, Herbert G. "The Chronology of Jeremiah's Oracles," *JNES* 4 (1945), 217–227.
Mays, James Luther and Achtemeier, Paul (eds.). *Interpreting the Prophets*. (Philadelphia: Fortress Press, 1987).

*Bibliography*

McKane, William. *Jeremiah I*. (ICC; Edinburgh: T. & T. Clark, 1986).
Meek, Theophile J. "Was Jeremiah a Priest?" *The Expositor* 8th Series 25 (1923), 215-222.
Michaelis, Christian B. *Prolegomena in Ieremiam Prophetam*. (Halle: Litteris Hendelianis, 1733).
Michaelis, Johann David. *Observationes Philologicae et Criticae in Jeremiae Vaticinia et Threnos*. (Göttingen: Vandenhoeck & Ruprecht, 1793).
Milgrom, Jacob. "The Date of Jeremiah, Chapter 2," *JNES* 14 (1955), 65-69.
Mowinckel, Sigmund. *Zur Komposition des Buches Jeremia*. (Oslo: Jacob Dybwad, 1914).
―――. *Prophecy and Tradition*. (Oslo: Jacob Dybwad, 1946).
Muilenburg, James. "Jeremiah the Prophet" in *IDB* E-J, 823-835.
―――. "The 'Office' of the Prophet in Ancient Israel" in *The Bible in Modern Scholarship*. (ed. J. Philip Hyatt; Nashville: Abingdon Press, 1965), 74-97 [= Best 1984: 127-150].
―――. "Baruch the Scribe" in *Proclamation and Presence*. (eds. John I. Durham and J. R. Porter; Richmond: John Knox Press, 1970), 215-238 [= Best 1984: 259-282; also Perdue and Kovacs 1984: 229-245].
Nicholson, E. W. *Preaching to the Exiles: A Study of the Prose Tradition in the Book of Jeremiah*. (New York: Schocken Books, 1971).
―――. *The Book of the Prophet Jeremiah Chapters 1-25*. (CBC; Cambridge: Cambridge University Press, 1973).
―――. *The Book of the Prophet Jeremiah Chapters 26-52*. (CBC; Cambridge: Cambridge University Press, 1975).
Nötscher, Fredrich. *Das Buch Jeremias*. (Bonn: Peter Hanstein Verlagsbuchhandlung, 1934).
Noth, Martin (ed.). *Essays in Honour of Millar Burrows*. (Leiden: E. J. Brill, 1959).
von Orelli, C. *The Prophecies of Jeremiah*. (tr. J. S. Banks; Edinburgh: T. & T. Clark, 1889).
Overholt, Thomas W. "Some Reflections on the Date of Jeremiah's Call," *CBQ* 33 (1971), 165-184.
Peake, A. S. *Jeremiah I*. (CB; New York: Henry Frowde, and Edinburgh: T. C. & E. C. Jack, 1910).
―――. *Jeremiah and Lamentations II*. (CB; New York: Henry Frowde, and Edinburgh: T. C. & E. C. Jack, 1911).
Perdue, Leo G. and Kovacs, Brian W. (eds.). *A Prophet to the Nations: Essays in Jeremiah Studies*. (Winona Lake, IN: Eisenbrauns, 1984).
Robinson, T. H. *Prophecy and the Prophets in Ancient Israel*. (London: Duckworth, 1923).
Rowley, H. H. "The Prophet Jeremiah and the Book of Deuteronomy" in *Studies in Old Testament Prophecy*. (ed. H. H. Rowley; Edinburgh: T. & T. Clark, 1950), 157-174.
―――. "The Early Prophecies of Jeremiah in Their Setting," *BJRL* 45 (1962-63), 198-234 [= Perdue and Kovacs 1984: 33-61].

*Bibliography*

Rudolph, Wilhelm. *Jeremia*. 3rd ed. (HAT; Tübingen: J. C. B. Mohr [Paul Siebeck], 1968).

Skinner, John. *Prophecy and Religion*. (Cambridge: Cambridge University Press, 1922).

Smith, George Adam. *Jeremiah*. 4th ed. (New York and London: Harper & Bros., 1929).

Streane, A. W. *The Book of the Prophet Jeremiah together with the Lamentations*. (CBSC; Cambridge: Cambridge University Press, 1913).

Thiel, Winfried. *Die deuteronomistische Redaktion von Jeremia 1–25*. (WMANT 41; Neukirchen-Vluyn: Neukirchener Verlag, 1973).

———. *Die deuteronomistische Redaktion von Jeremia 26–45*. (WMANT 52; Neukirchen-Vluyn: Neukirchener Verlag, 1981).

Thompson, J. A. *The Book of Jeremiah*. (NICOT; Grand Rapids: William B. Eerdmans Publishing Co., 1980).

Torrey, C. C. "The Background of Jeremiah 1–10," *JBL* 56 (1937). 193–216.

Volz, D. Paul. *Der Prophet Jeremia*. 2nd ed. (KAT; Leipzig: A. Deichertsche Verlagsbuchhandlung, D. Werner Scholl, 1928).

Weinfeld, Moshe. "Deuteronomy—The Present State of Inquiry," *JBL* 86 (1967), 249–262 (= D. Christensen ed. A Song of Power and the Power of Song; Winona Lake, IN: Eisenbrauns 1993, 21–35).

———. *Deuteronomy and the Deuteronomic School*. (Oxford: Clarendon Press, 1972).

Weiser, Artur. *Das Buch Jeremia 1–25,13*. 8th ed. (ATD 20; Göttingen: Vandenhoeck & Ruprecht, 1981). Originally 1952.

Welch, Adam C. *Jeremiah: His Time and His Work*. (Oxford: Oxford University Press, and London: Humphrey Milford, 1928 [reprint Westport, CT: Greenwood Press, 1980]).

———. *The Work of the Chronicler*. (London: British Academy and Oxford University Press, 1939).

Wellhausen, Julius. *Prolegomenon to the History of Ancient Israel*. (New York and Cleveland: World Publishing Co., 1957). Originally 1878.

Whitley, C. F. "The Date of Jeremiah's Call," *VT* 14 (1964), 467–483 [= Perdue and Kovacs 1984: 73–87].

Wilke, Fritz. "Das Skythenproblem im Jeremiabuch" in *Alttestamentliche Studien*, BWAT 13 (Leipzig: J. C. Hinrichs'sche Buchhandlung, 1913), 222–254.

Winckler, Hugo. *Geschichte Israels I*. (Leipzig: Verlag von Eduard Pfeiffer, 1895).

Wright, G. Ernest. "The Lawsuit of God: A Form-Critical Study of Deuteronomy 32" in *Israel's Prophetic Heritage*. (eds. Bernhard W. Anderson and Walter Harrelson; New York: Harper and Bros., 1962), 26–67.

Wright, G. E. and Freedman, David Noel (eds.). *The Biblical Archaeologist Reader*. (Garden City, NY: Doubleday and Co., 1961 [= Ann Arbor: American Schools of Oriental Research, 1978]).

Young, E. J. *An Introduction to the Old Testament*. (Grand Rapids: Wm. B. Eerdmans Publishing Co., 1954).

# Scripture Index

## Genesis

| | |
|---|---|
| 1 | 78 |
| 18:22–33 | 78 |
| 37:2 | 5 |

## Exodus

| | |
|---|---|
| 2:11–22 | 58 |
| 2:11 | 58 |
| 3–4 | 46 |
| 3:1–14 | 71 |
| 3:1–6 | 59 |
| 4:10–17 | 58 |

## Deuteronomy

| | |
|---|---|
| 1–28 | 69, 72, 75 |
| 1:5 | 73 |
| 4:30 | 77 |
| 4:44 | 73 |
| 5:26, 28 | 18 |
| 10:16 | 77 |
| 12–26 | 18 |
| 12:1–7 | 30 |
| 13:1–5 | 82 |
| 18:15 | 46 |
| 18:18 | 46, 47, 51, 63, 70 |
| 24:1–4 | 21, 46, 51 |
| 27 | 25 |
| 27:26 | 25 |
| 28 | 26 |
| 29–34 | 73 |
| 31:9–13 | 49 |
| 31:24 | 72 |
| 31:26 | 73 |
| 32 | 18, 47, 51, 64 |
| 32:10–18 | 75 |
| 32:15–22 | 72 |
| 32:46 | 73 |
| 34:10–12 | 70 |

## Joshua

| | |
|---|---|
| 18:23 | 13 |

## 1 Samuel

| | |
|---|---|
| 2:11 | 58 |
| 2:18 | 58 |
| 2:21 | 58 |
| 2:26 | 58 |
| 3:1 | 58 |
| 3:8 | 58 |

## 1 Kings

| | |
|---|---|
| 2:26–27 | 67 |
| 3:7 | 5 |

## 2 Kings

| | |
|---|---|
| 18:1–6 | 70 |
| 21:19—23:37 | 7 |
| 22–23 | 2, 8, 18 |
| 22 | 32 |
| 22:3–14 | 44 |
| 22:8 | 44 |

## Scripture Index

| | |
|---|---|
| 22:12 | 44 |
| 22:13 | 48 |
| 22:16–20 | 72 |
| 23 | 23 |
| 23:8 | 69 |
| 23:9 | 74 |
| 23:15–18/20 | 49 |
| 23:21–23 | 73 |
| 23:23 | 69 |
| 23:25 | 72 |
| 23:31–34 | 80 |
| 23:34 | 11 |

### 2 Chronicles

| | |
|---|---|
| 28:16–21 | 10 |
| 29–31 | 70 |
| 34–35 | 8, 18 |
| 34:3 | 5 |
| 34:3a | 69 |
| 34:3b–7 | 18, 67 |
| 34:14 | 72 |
| 35:1–19 | 73 |
| 35:20–22 | 81 |
| 35:25 | 5, 41, 80 |

### Job

| | |
|---|---|
| 2:13 | 61 |

### Psalms

| | |
|---|---|
| 78:60 | 68 |
| 119:103 | 63 |

### Isaiah

| | |
|---|---|
| 6 | 59 |
| 6:1 | 47, 71 |
| 6:8 | 59 |
| 8:16–17 | 3 |

### Jeremiah

| | |
|---|---|
| 1–25 | 51 |
| 1–20 | xi, 5, 8, 22, 31, 40, 49, 54, 55, 83 |
| 1–10 | 19, 22 |
| 1–6 | 19, 22 |
| 1–2 | 22 |
| 1 | 1, 6, 38, 54, 57, 59, 61, 62, 63, 64 |
| 1:1–3 | 2 |
| 1:1–2 | 1, 41 |
| 1:1 | 42 |
| 1:2 | xi, 2, 5, 41, 42, 43, 44, 45, 47, 51, 52, 56, 62, 66 |
| 1:4–12 | 54, 58 |
| 1:4–10 | 2, 6, 44, 46, 51, 57, 62 |
| 1:4 | 2, 5, 44, 48, 52, 56, 57, 62 |
| 1:5 | 44, 52 |
| 1:6–7 | 5, 6 |
| 1:6 | 58 |
| 1:7 | 46, 64 |
| 1:8 | 61, 65 |
| 1:9 | 47, 59, 61, 62, 63, 64, 72 |
| 1:10 | 65, 73 |
| 1:11–16 | 6, 56 |
| 1:11–12 | 57 |
| 1:11 | 6, 48, 56, 57 |
| 1:12 | 57, 59, 64 |
| 1:13–19 | 33, 58, 64, 74 |
| 1:13–15 | 33, 38 |
| 1:13–14 | 35, 57 |
| 1:13 | 48, 56, 57, 64 |
| 1:14–19 | 55, 56 |
| 1:15–19 | 57 |
| 1:15 | 38, 57 |
| 1:16 | 57, 61 |
| 1:17–19 | 6, 64 |
| 1:17 | 57, 64, 65 |
| 1:18–19 | 61 |
| 1:18 | 57 |

## Scripture Index

| | | | |
|---|---|---|---|
| 1:19 | 57, 65 | 4:2a | 23 |
| 2–6 | 19 | 4:3b | 19 |
| 2–3 | 13, 19, 20 | 4:5—6:30 | 22, 33, 36, 37, 38, 78 |
| 2 | 11, 22, 47, 51, 64 | 4:5–8 | 33, 34 |
| 2:1—4:4 | 22, 49, 75 | 4:5 | 33 |
| 2:1 | 56 | 4:6 | 33 |
| 2:2–3 | 9, 28, 75 | 4:9–10 | 79 |
| 2:5–13 | 20, 21 | 4:23–26 | 78 |
| 2:5–9 | 75 | 5:1–8 | 78 |
| 2:8 | 29, 77 | 5:1 | 24 |
| 2:13 | 11 | 5:4–5 | 29, 77 |
| 2:8 | 77 | 5:12–13 | 79 |
| 2:14–19 | 8, 9, 11, 41 | 5:15 | 38 |
| 2:14–17 | 11 | 5:20–31 | 79 |
| 2:15 | 9 | 6 | 22 |
| 2:16 | 9, 11, 41 | 6:1 | 33 |
| 2:18 | 8, 10, 11, 12, 13, 76 | 6:13–15 | 79 |
| 2:36 | 8, 11, 12, 76 | 6:16–21 | 28, 31, 39, 79 |
| 3–6 | 22 | 6:16 | 28 |
| 3 | 21, 27 | 6:17 | 39 |
| 3:1 | 21, 22, 46, 51 | 6:22–26 | 34, 35 |
| 3:6–13 | 17 | 6:22 | 33 |
| 3:6–11 | 17, 79 | 7 | 22, 45 |
| 3:6 | 4, 5, 17, 40, 42, 43 | 7:1–15 | 75, 81 |
| 3:12–18 | 16 | 7:3–7 | 75 |
| 3:12–15 | 28 | 7:8–11 | 75 |
| 3:12–14 | 16 | 7:12–15 | 75 |
| 3:12–13/14 | 28 | 7:22–23 | 30 |
| 3:12–13 | 16, 17, 76 | 7:31 | 31 |
| 3:14–18 | 17 | 8–10 | 78, 80 |
| 3:14–15 | 17 | 8 | 33 |
| 3:14 | 17, 28, 76 | 8:4—9:22[21] | 78 |
| 3:14b | 28 | 8:4–13 | 50 |
| 3:15 | 17 | 8:4–7 | 79 |
| 3:16–18 | 17 | 8:8–9 | 28, 29, 30, 31 |
| 3:18 | 17 | 8:8 | 31, 77 |
| 3:21–25 | 80 | 8:8ab | 29 |
| 4 | 22 | 8:8b | 29 |
| 4:1–4 | 22, 23, 76, 77 | 8:10b–12 | 79 |
| 4:1–2 | 75 | 8:13–17 | 78 |
| | | 8:18–21 | 78 |

## Scripture Index

| Reference | Page | Reference | Page |
|---|---|---|---|
| 8:22—9:2[1] | 78 | 15:17 | 61, 73 |
| 9:10–11[9–10] | 78 | 15:18 | 72 |
| 10:17–22 | 78 | 15:19–21 | 61, 79, 80 |
| 10:22 | 33 | 15:19–20 | 61 |
| 10:23–24 | 80 | 15:19 | 61 |
| 11–20 | 55, 80 | 15:20 | 61 |
| 11 | 26 | 16:1–9 | 78 |
| 11:1–17 | 27, 40 | 17:19–27 | 76 |
| 11:1–16 | 50 | 18:18 | 29 |
| 11:1–8 | 23, 24, 27, 30, 76 | 19 | 82 |
| 11:1–6 | 27 | 19:5 | 31 |
| 11:1–5 | 24 | 20:1–6 | 82 |
| 11:2–3 | 25 | 20:7–18 | 82 |
| 11:2 | 24 | 20:7–10 | 80 |
| 11:3–5 | 25 | 20:11–13 | 80 |
| 11:4–5 | 25 | 20:14–18 | 80 |
| 11:6–8 | 25 | 20:15 | 68 |
| 11:6b | 26 | 21–45 | xvi |
| 11:7 | 25 | 22:10–12 | 80 |
| 11:8 | 25, 26 | 22:13–17 | 81, 82 |
| 11:8b | 26, 27 | 23:9–40 | 82 |
| 11:9–17 | 23 | 24:1–10 | 58 |
| 11:9 | 23 | 25 | 1 |
| 11:10 | 23 | 25:1–3 | 2, 66 |
| 11:14–17 | 80 | 25:1 | 45 |
| 11:18—12:6 | 77 | 25:3 | 4, 41, 42, 43 |
| 13:1–11 | 12, 76 | 25:9 | 83 |
| 13:4 | 13 | 26 | 45 |
| 13:5 | 13 | 26:1 | 81 |
| 13:6 | 13 | 26:20–23 | 82 |
| 13:7 | 13 | 26:24 | 32, 44, 71, 82 |
| 13:15–27 | 14 | 29:3 | 32, 44, 71 |
| 14:1–9 | 80 | 30–31 | 8, 14, 16, 17, 27, 31, 40, 49 |
| 14:11–12 | 80 | 30:2 | 71 |
| 14:19–22 | 80 | 30:10 | 14 |
| 15:1–4 | 80 | 30:18 | 14 |
| 15:15–21 | 59, 60, 65 | 31 | 16 |
| 15:15–18 | 80 | 31:2–20 | 76 |
| 15:16–17 | 58, 59, 62, 63 | 31:2–14 | 14–16, 76 |
| 15:16 | 47, 48, 61, 63, 73 | 31:6 | 27 |
| 15:16a | 51 | 31:7 | 14 |

| | | | |
|---|---|---|---|
| 31:8 | 14 | **Hosea** | |
| 31:9 | 14 | | |
| 31:10–14 | 27 | 7:11 | 10 |
| 31:11 | 14 | | |
| 31:12 | 27 | **Amos** | |
| 31:18 | 14 | | |
| 31:20 | 14 | 7:1–9 | 58 |
| 32:6–9 | 67 | 7:10–13 | 81 |
| 35 | 50, 82 | | |
| 36 | 49 | **Jonah** | |
| 36:1–8 | 83 | | |
| 36:1–2 | 66 | 3 | 76 |
| 36:2 | 4, 42, 43, 71 | | |
| 36:9–32 | 83 | **Habakkuk** | |
| 36:9–26 | 3 | | |
| 36:9 | 2 | 1:5–11 | 83 |
| 36:10–12 | 44 | | |
| 36:11–12 | 71 | **Zephaniah** | |
| 36:19 | 3, 50 | | |
| 36:25 | 71 | 2:1–4 | 69 |
| 36:26 | 3, 50 | | |
| 39:14 | 32, 44, 71 | **Zechariah** | |
| 40:5–6 | 71 | | |
| 41:5 | 14, 27 | 10:10–11 | 41 |
| 45 | 83 | | |
| 46:3–12 | 82 | **Revelation** | |
| 47:2–7 | 83 | | |
| 51:60 | | 10:8–11 | 63 |
| 71 | | | |

## Ezekiel

| | |
|---|---|
| 1–3 | 59 |
| 2:8—3:3 | 48, 61 |
| 3:3 | 63 |
| 3:14 | 61, 63 |
| 3:15 | 61 |
| 16 | 17, 40 |
| 23 | 17, 40 |

www.ingramcontent.com/pod-product-compliance
Lightning Source LLC
Chambersburg PA
CBHW050842160426
43192CB00011B/2123